Holy Spirit

SUPERNATURAL POWER
FOR LIFE AND MINISTRY

STEVE EVANS

forerunner
MINISTRIES

forerunner
PUBLISHING
Savannah, Georgia

Holy Spirit: Supernatural Power for Life and Ministry
2015 by Steve Evans

Distributed by Forerunner Ministries, Inc.
   4625 Sussex Place, Savannah, GA 31405
   Email: **steve@forerunners4him.org**
   Website: **www.forerunners4him.org**

Published by Forerunner Ministries, Inc.
ISBN-13: 978-0692464281 (Forerunner)
ISBN-10: 069246428X

Cover and interior design by Forerunner Publishing, Savannah, Georgia.

Printed in the United States of America by CreateSpace.

TABLE OF CONTENTS

Holy Spirit

SPIRIT LED LIVING

For all who are led by the Spirit of God are sons of God.
Romans 8:14 ESV

CHAPTER 1

HOSTING A MYSTERY

The Holy Spirit has been with us all our lives and we may never have known it. Never once have sensed His Presence or felt His touch in any recognizable way. That all ends now! Let this book give you eyes to see and ears to hear. We are on the hunt to discover all we can about this very reclusive Quarry. Fortunately, there are clues scattered all over scripture showing us ways to track Him down, draw near, and join hands with our perpetually present God. Still it must be admitted our interior Guest is quite a Mystery. Simply being God is mystery enough!

For who knows a person's thoughts except the spirit of that person, which is in him? So also no one comprehends the thoughts of God except the Spirit of God. 1 Corinthians 2:11-12

The Holy Spirit is God all by Himself, but He is never just by Himself—He is inseparably "at one" with the other two Persons of the Trinity. This compounds the mystery. Everything *as God* that is true of Them is, therefore, also true of the Holy Spirit.[1] Nevertheless, though the Father is visibly described twice in the scriptures[2] and Jesus has been seen many times and in many ways, no one is reported to have "seen" the Spirit. That we will all see the Father and Jesus once we are in heaven is beyond question. Whether or not we will ever see the Spirit is anyone's guess. This stretches our present Mystery way into the future.

One further difficulty in writing about the Holy Spirit is that He doesn't like to draw attention to Himself, preferring to focus our eyes on Jesus and the Father instead. He who is more powerful than Niagara Falls is also more elusive than a vapor mirage on a hot summer highway. That makes it all the more fun! Let's seek to discover just who this Mystery Person is and how it is that He enables us to live the Christian life with so much joy and supernatural empowerment. Come along, as we lift the curtain to catch revealing glimpses of our secretive Companion.

Holy Spirit

CHAPTER 2

HOLY SPIRIT OUR HELPER

Jesus said He would not leave us comfortless and He hasn't. He is living in us through the Holy Spirit who is "sealed" to us a sign of our eternal destiny and as a present source of help and hope for any situation of need we may encounter.[1] Because He is holy He shows us what doesn't belong in us (sin). Because He is wholly good he helps us in the most patient, loving ways imaginable as He works to lead us out of our darkness into the full Light of Christ. All the while He draws so little attention to Himself, you would hardly know He is there.

Nevertheless, I tell you the truth: it is to your advantage that I go away, for if I do not go away, the Helper will not come to you.
John 16:7

Help on the Inside

Jesus said that He would send the Holy Spirit to be our "Helper." This has been wildly misunderstood with people thinking that only Christians "have" the Holy Spirit or that the Holy Spirit only came to help people after the resurrection. God has always and will always be doing things for us by the Holy Spirit. That is nothing new.[2]

The Holy Spirit did all kinds of great things for Jewish believers in the Old Testament. He does great things for everyone who calls on the Lord and always has. Not only that, He has always been the giver and sustainer of life for everyone and every creature in creation, regardless of whether they know Him or not.[3] None of this has changed through anything that Jesus did for us by His death and resurrection. What did change?

To them God chose to make known how great among the Gentiles are the riches of the glory of this mystery, which is Christ in you, the hope of glory. Colossians 1:27

The altogether new thing that God is doing for us is that the Holy Spirit now lives inside all who give their lives to Christ through faith-conversion and the new birth.[4] This (along with Christ's sacrifice) makes the "new and living way" possible.[5] The Holy Spirit lives inside of us as our Helper, helping us to live in a "new way" that was never before possible outside of childhood—the way of surrender and trust.[6]

Before we became Christians, the Holy Spirit our Helper was always doing things for us, even if we didn't know it, but now that we are Christians, He is helping us from the inside to live through Him.[7] Faith conversion helps us in two tremendous ways. We can call on the Lord with confidence that God by His Spirit will do for us more than we can ask or think.[8] We can also call on the Lord for His help in surrendering so that God can live *through* us in ways He never could before.[9]

A New Way of Life

Naturally, God will go on doing things for us. He always has. The missing element—the part the "sending" of the Holy Spirit is intended to correct—is that now we can truly live for God by trusting Jesus and obeying Jesus with the Holy Spirit *helping us on the inside*. By indwelling us the Holy Spirit is able to help us live as we were always meant to live with real joy, peace, freedom and faithfulness.

By all means, keep on thinking of God as "out there" and "up there," but add to that "in here." Think of Him as willing to work for you, but think also of Him as wanting to live through you. If you are in Christ through faith, then the Holy Spirit is in you, working, working, working to help you learn how to live in and with and through His inner Life.

Your new personality, for instance, looks just like His. Deep down you have been joined to Him and have been given a new heart just like that of Jesus.[10] This means, that although the old heart of the old nature will still be throwing up all kinds of negative emotions, false beliefs and wrong desires for you to contend with, you have a choice that was never available to you before. Now that you know who Jesus is, you can choose (by your new heart) to cling to Him

10

and call on Him for help to break free of the old ways.[11] This "new and living way" works best when we trust Jesus enough to obey Him step by step. That may seem like a tall order, but the Holy Spirit will work inside you to help you with this. That's His new assignment.

In any moment in which you choose to surrender your life and your choices to Jesus, the Holy Spirit's "personality" will emerge inside you. Not perfectly perhaps, but very wonderfully, filling you to the degree that you yield yourself to God. What then begins to flow is peace, love, joy, and all sorts of good things.[12] This is the mighty river of the new life which Jesus said would flow out of the heart of all who believe in Him.[13] But there is a catch. Just believing in who Jesus is will not be enough to get you into the river most days. You have to believe in Him enough to trust Him with what He allows and follow Him in what He asks.

The great way it feels and the God ordained things that keep happening are powerful incentives to keep surrendering to Jesus and flowing in the "river of peace."[14] Jesus said that believing in Him (at this level of trust) is "the work" you and I are required and expected to do by our God.[15] That is why He has put His Spirit inside of us—to help us with the work of staying surrendered and submitted to Him no matter what is going on around us.

The Inner Witness

The Holy Spirit helps us by being an Inner Witness. He is always reminding us that Jesus is alive and that He is our Savior and Lord.[16] Even the most backslidden Christians still have this inner witness quietly at work on the inside reminding them of the direction they need to turn. Once He sees we are willing to turn, the Holy Spirit will help us pray, reminding us to cling to and call on Jesus. This is absolutely essential!

Until we start calling on Jesus in a situation of trouble or temptation, we are actually calling on ourselves. "Self" will never be a sufficient savior.[17] Leaning on yourself always leads to stress, anxiety, depression and fresh disasters. The new life is leaning hard on Jesus, clinging to Him and calling on Him. This activity on the inside does more than anything else to change us from being self-centered creations of our own self-will, to Christ-centered new creations filled with His Spirit.

The Holy Spirit helps as a "Remembrancer," reminding us what we have already been taught.[18] The enemy seeks to steal out of our hearts the Word that God sows. Holy Spirit works to keep God's truths in our remembrance. (Hint: You can make His work easier by memorizing key scriptures.) Holy Spirit is also our "Revealer of Truth," leading us out of our darkness into Christ's Light.

And when he comes, he will convict the world concerning sin and righteousness and judgment: concerning sin, because they do not believe in me; concerning righteousness, because I go to the Father, and you will see me no longer; concerning judgment, because the ruler of this world is judged. John 16:8-11

Because we all have such a hard time recognizing what may be wrong about things we habitually believe and do, Holy Spirit is our inner guide to what's true, convicting us of sin (showing us what's wrong), and convincing us of righteousness (what is good and right from God's point of view). He also helps us by reminding us of judgment. Just as the enemy will be judged and have to face the full consequences of all the wrong he has done, so our own wrong doing will bring down consequences on us unless we separate from them in time. [19] That gives us plenty of motivation!

In all these ways and more, the Holy Spirit points us to Christ, working to help us trust Jesus with what He allows and with all that He asks. As we release our cares, the Holy Spirit raises us into the peace of Christ, shows us the next right thing to do, and then helps us do it. All of this, of course, depends on our willingness.[20] But the Holy Spirit will even help us with that—if we want Him to. Learn this prayer, inviting the Holy Spirit to work in your heart, especially at those times when you sense that you don't want to surrender to God: "Lord, help me want to want what You want, desire what You desire, and hate what You hate." Give Holy Spirit permission to go to work! His help will make your job of following Jesus step by step so much easier to accomplish.

CHAPTER 3

NEW LIFE IN THE SPIRIT

There are two sides to salvation: Jesus' death <u>for</u> you and the Spirit's life <u>in</u> you. Just as Jesus died for you the death you deserved, so the Holy Spirit has come to live in and through you the life you could not attain. As you look to Jesus in love and trust, the Holy Spirit (without any effort on your part) raises you into the new way of life. Walking in the Spirit is a great beginning; supernatural empowerment lies just ahead.

And Peter said to them, "Repent and be baptized every one of you in the name of Jesus Christ for the forgiveness of your sins, and you will receive the gift of the Holy Spirit." Acts 2:38

Two Tremendous Promises

During the Old Testament period the Holy Spirit was definitely present and powerful, but He was never permanently present within the Israelite believers, nor was His power equally available to them all. A few individuals, for instance, were chosen and anointed by the Spirit of God for specific reasons. Prophets, priest, kings, leaders like the "judge" Samson, craftsmen, and others experienced the Holy Spirit coming "upon" them at certain times or were "anointed" for certain tasks.

God promised that this would change dramatically in the future. The day would surely come when the Lord God would make a way for His Spirit to be placed both "within" and also be poured out "upon" his believing people.

1) Inward Life. The promise of an indwelling presence was given through Ezekiel. The Lord declared that one day He would give us a "new heart" and put a "new spirit" *within* us. In hindsight we can see better what this meant than would have been possible for Ezekiel's contemporaries. Through faith-conversion we now understand that God gives us a new heart—one that knows Him

13

and loves Him—*and* places His Spirit within us when we are born again. This is called regeneration and it is accomplished as the Holy Spirit is joined to our spirit, raising us from spiritual death to new life in Christ. So much of this hidden work is shrouded in mysteries that we may never fully understand or agree upon. Nevertheless, it is clear even in this prophetic passage from Ezekiel that God intends to cleanse us from sin and restore us to faithful living by empowering us from within.

> **"I will sprinkle clean water on you, and you shall be clean from all your uncleannesses, and from all your idols I will cleanse you. And I will give you a new heart, and a new spirit I will put within you."**
> Ezekiel 36:25-26

2) Supernatural Power. The promise of an empowering presence was given through Joel. The Lord declared that one day He would "pour out" the Holy Spirit *upon* us. In the words of Joel this outpouring would be upon "all flesh"—not just a select few. Everyone in the faith community from youth to elderly, both men and women, would be suitable candidates for receiving this divine empowerment. Dreams, visions and prophecy are specifically identified as among the supernatural gifts that would be given, but more is implied. The prophets of ancient Israel were renowned, not just for their visionary encounters with God and their words from the Lord, but also for healing and miracles of all kinds. These too will be "poured out" when the Holy Spirit comes upon God's people to empower them for supernatural works of ministry.

In the Upper Room on the evening of the Resurrection as Jesus breathed upon His disciples, they "received" the Holy Spirit. Clearly, at this moment in time they were the first fully "born again" believers in the resurrected Lord.[1] This fulfilled the Father's promise given through Ezekiel.

> **And when he had said this, he breathed on them and said to them, "Receive the Holy Spirit. If you forgive the sins of anyone, they are forgiven; if you withhold forgiveness from anyone, it is withheld."**
> John 20:22-23

In the Upper Room on the morning of Pentecost (50 days later) many of these same disciples received the outpouring of the Holy Spirit upon them. This fulfilled the Father's promise of empowerment given through Joel, which is also the "promise of the Father" Jesus referred to when He told them to pray and wait for "power from on high."[2]

When the day of Pentecost arrived, they were all together in one place. And suddenly there came from heaven a sound like a mighty rushing wind, and it filled the entire house where they were sitting. And divided tongues as of fire appeared to them and rested on each one of them. And they were all filled with the Holy Spirit and began to speak in other tongues as the Spirit gave them utterance. Acts 2:1-4

Two Ways to Receive the Gift

What this tells us is that there are two quite different ways in which the Holy Spirit can be given to those who believe. These gifts equip us in different ways for different purposes.

1) Every Christian receives the gift of the indwelling presence of the Holy Spirit within them through faith-conversion when they repent and turn to Jesus as their Savior. This is the source of our new life in Christ. We are forgiven for our past and we have Jesus living in us through the Holy Spirit. We all receive an equipping for dwelling in Jesus by faith and growing spiritual fruit as we learn to trust and obey Him.

2) Any Christian who desires it can also receive the gift of the outpouring of the Holy Spirit upon them. This baptism of power is the source of our empowerment for the supernatural workings of the Holy Spirit. We can receive an equipping for Jesus to do His deeds of power through us by His Holy Spirit. Being "baptized with power" from on high is available to everyone who believes in the Risen Lord and is willing to seek this further blessing and empowerment.

Holy Spirit

CHAPTER 4

HOLY SPIRIT, JESUS AND YOU

The family resemblance is uncanny. Jesus' earthly relationship with the Holy Spirit is exactly mirrored by our own, practically in every detail. The few remaining parts of the image require our trusting obedience to fill in. Will we allow God to finish the portrait He desires to paint upon the canvass of our life?

"A disciple is not above his teacher, nor a servant above his master. It is enough for the disciple to be like his teacher, and the servant like his master." Matthew 10:24-25

Jesus our Example

The unnamed writer of Hebrews tells us that in order to save us from sin-bondage, death and temptation, Jesus had to be made like us "in every respect."[1] The Eternal Son of God became fully human in order to be both our representative at the cross and our example for how to live the new life He would give us. This radical descent of God into His creation never fails to astonish, whenever we pause to consider what it must have meant for Jesus to become like us. But there is a "flip side" to the Redemption which Jesus' descent accomplished: what it means *for us*. Through faith-conversion have now been "raised up" into being "like" Him.

If then you have been raised with Christ, seek the things that are above, where Christ is, seated at the right hand of God. Set your minds on things that are above, not on things that are on earth. For you have died, and your life is hidden with Christ in God.
Colossians 3:1-3

At the very least the above passage should clue us in that many things about us are radically changed from what we might have imagined ourselves to be like—based on our past (earth-bound) experience and understanding of ourselves. Now that Jesus is "in us" and we are "in Him" all bets are off! We can only truly know ourselves and our world from Christ's perspective. Since that perspective is heavenly it is guaranteed to be a) filled with delight and b) incredibly strange.

Get ready to re-adjust your thinking about yourself by seeing what scripture has to say about you, now that you have received Jesus as your indwelling Savior and Redeemer. Some of the following seven likenesses have already been accomplished at your conversion. Some will require your willing participation to enter more fully into the mystery and power of new life. Whatever you decide to do, don't hold back.[2] No one loves you better or has greater joy planned for you than Jesus. See what He has done for you and let that be both recommendation and invitation to follow Him further into the dynamic union that He desires.

> "I in them and you in me, that they may become perfectly one, so that the world may know that you sent me and loved them even as you loved me." John 17:23

Our Likeness to Jesus in the Holy Spirit

1) Born of the Holy Spirit

> And Mary said to the angel, "How will this be, since I am a virgin?" And the angel answered her, "The Holy Spirit will come upon you, and the power of the Most High will overshadow you; therefore the child to be born will be called holy— the Son of God. Luke 1:34-36

Jesus was born of the Holy Spirit. The miracle of His birth sets the pattern for our re-birth: Jesus of Nazareth is truly the flesh and blood child of Mary; He is also from conception the Eternal Son of our heavenly Father. It was the Holy Spirit who accomplished this. Now it is our turn, if we are willing to turn back to God. Just as Jesus was born from above by the sinless Spirit of God, so, too, we creatures of flesh and blood are born from above by the same Holy Spirit.

> Jesus answered, "Truly, truly, I say to you, unless one is born of water and the Spirit, he cannot enter the kingdom of God. That which is

born of the flesh is flesh, and that which is born of the Spirit is spirit. Do not marvel that I said to you, 'You must be born again.'" John 3:5-7

2) Filled with the Holy Spirit

For he whom God has sent utters the words of God, for he gives the Spirit without measure. The Father loves the Son and has given all things into his hand. John 3:34-35

Just as Jesus was filled with the Holy Spirit without measure, so, too, are we. It is immensely comforting to know (by faith) that God gives His Spirit to us "without measure." Otherwise it could easily seem that we only got a very tiny portion, since what we usually sense of the Lord's presence with us may seem fairly slight. There is a huge difference, however, between the Holy Spirit's actual presence and His manifest Presence. Holy Spirit is always in us in fullness, though we may not sense any manifestation of His Presence. Part of our high calling is to press in to this Reality through faith so that (experientially) we can be filled with the fullness that lies within.

So that Christ may dwell in your hearts through faith—that you, being rooted and grounded in love, may have strength to comprehend with all the saints what is the breadth and length and height and depth, and to know the love of Christ that surpasses knowledge, that you may be filled with all the fullness of God. Ephesians 3:17-19

3) Baptized with the Holy Spirit

And when Jesus was baptized, immediately he went up from the water, and behold, the heavens were opened to him, and he saw the Spirit of God descending like a dove and coming to rest on him. Matthew 3:16

Immediately after being baptized with water, Jesus was baptized with the Holy Spirit. Jesus didn't need faith-conversion or water baptism to be cleansed of sin as we do, but He submitted to it as an act of obedience.[3] Our faith-conversion and water baptism "catch us up" with Him for the new birth and the indwelling Spirit provide us with a sinless nature united with God just as Jesus enjoyed from birth. The one piece that still needs to fall into place is the baptism in the Spirit. Jesus received it immediately; most of us don't. According to Jesus' own words, we are to pray and seek this further experience of empowerment.

> **And while staying with them he ordered them not to depart from Jerusalem, but to wait for the promise of the Father, which, he said, "you heard from me; for John baptized with water, but you will be baptized with the Holy Spirit not many days from now." Acts 1:4-5**

4) Led by the Holy Spirit

> **Then Jesus was led up by the Spirit into the wilderness to be tempted by the devil. Matthew 4:1**

Immediately after being baptized, Jesus was led by the Holy Spirit into the wilderness. There was nothing accidental about this: Jesus was following a clear leading of the Spirit. Since Jesus explained elsewhere that He always did what He saw the Father doing, being led by the Spirit was something Jesus had been practicing consciously all His life.[4] Naturally, we have some catching up to do here. Sometimes the leading of the Holy Spirit will be without our conscious knowing; at other times it will seem to depend entirely upon our willing participation. Nevertheless, whether it is conscious or un-conscious, we are now being led by the same Holy Spirit who led Jesus!

> **For all who are led by the Spirit of God are sons of God. Romans 8:14**

5) Sealed by the Holy Spirit

> **"Do not labor for the food that perishes, but for the food that endures to eternal life, which the Son of Man will give to you. For on him God the Father has set his seal." John 6:27**

The Father set His seal upon Jesus. In the ancient world the seal was an authoritative sign, representing ownership or origin. Documents were sealed as a declaration of the sender's identity and as a guarantee that what they conveyed was an authentic expression of his will. We, too, have received a seal set upon us by the Father as a guarantee that everything He has promised will come to pass for those who desire to enter into this New Covenant. Just as ancient seals also proclaimed ownership of goods, we have been sealed as a sign of our belonging to Jesus, body, soul and spirit.

> **In him you also, when you heard the word of truth, the gospel of your salvation, and believed in him, were sealed with the promised Holy Spirit, who is the guarantee of our inheritance until we acquire possession of it, to the praise of his glory.** Ephesians 1:13-14

6) Empowered by the Holy Spirit

> **And Jesus returned in the power of the Spirit to Galilee, and a report about him went out through all the surrounding country. And he taught in their synagogues, being glorified by all.** Luke 4:14-15

Jesus lived and ministered in the power of the Holy Spirit. This was the secret of His effectiveness at teaching, healing and casting out demons.[5] God wants the same empowerment for us. A great deal of that power comes through the indwelling Spirit who enables us to recognize truth, witness about Christ, grow in the fruit of the Spirit and stand firm against temptation. What further power could we need? Power for the supernatural works that Jesus did![6] This kind of empowerment comes through the baptism of the Spirit. Significantly, it is this empowerment which Jesus commanded His recently born again converts to seek.

> **"But you will receive power when the Holy Spirit has come upon you, and you will be my witnesses in Jerusalem and in all Judea and Samaria, and to the end of the earth."** Acts 1:8

7) Anointed by the Holy Spirit

> **You yourselves know what happened throughout all Judea, beginning from Galilee after the baptism that John proclaimed: how God anointed Jesus of Nazareth with the Holy Spirit and with power. He went about doing good and healing all who were oppressed by the devil, for God was with him.** Acts 10:37-39

Prophets, priests and kings were anointed with oil in the Old Testament as a sign that the Holy Spirit would be working through them in their calling. The anointing was thus a sign of the Spirit's presence and power upon an individual for accomplishing things which they could not do by natural ability alone. Jesus lived under this anointing in every area of His life, including His capacity for joy and for setting captives free.[7] We get to follow Him in this! We are also anointed by the Holy Spirit to help us carry out our assignments. This anointing increases as we abide in Christ.

> **But the anointing that you received from him abides in you, and you have no need that anyone should teach you. But as his anointing teaches you about everything—and is true and is no lie, just as it has taught you—abide in him. 1 John 2:27**

Some "Unfinished" Business

Jesus sets the standard: He is our Model for ministry and Example for how to live. If He needed all of the above seven aspects of relationship with the Holy Spirit, why wouldn't we? Three of the seven have already been provided for us through faith-coversion: born by the Spirit, filled by the Spirit and sealed by the Spirit. Three have begun, but will need our intentional cultivation: being led by the Spirit, empowered by the Spirit and anointed by the Spirit. One will require deliberate seeking, if we are to receive it at all: the baptism of the Spirit. Jesus abided in God, doing whatever He "saw" the Father doing. In the same way we need to abide in Christ, doing everything we see Him doing.

CHAPTER 5

THE INDWELLING PRESENCE

Surprise! The Holy Spirit of God is now living inside of you! He has always been with you, but now He is in you. This is our guarantee that we are indeed going to heaven, but it is so much more.[1] Holy Spirit has been sent to bring into our lives everything necessary for new life and right living. It is impossible to live as a true Christian without God's help and we don't have to: The Helper is always as close as your next thought.

> **"And I will ask the Father, and he will give you another Helper, to be with you forever, even the Spirit of truth, whom the world cannot receive, because it neither sees him nor knows him. You know him, for he dwells with you and will be in you."** John 14:16-17

Did You Ask for This?

As part of our "birth from above" the gift of the indwelling presence of the Holy Spirit is automatic, involuntary and unheralded.[2] The Holy Spirit is given for free without our asking or our knowing. You could become a born again Christian without ever realizing that the Holy Spirit now lives inside you. This is partly because our focus in being saved is almost entirely upon Jesus, and mostly because the Holy Spirit rarely calls attention to Himself.[3]

The truth is that few people ever get saved because their primary desire is to receive the Holy Spirit. They aren't even thinking about the Holy Spirit. Once saved, their eyes are on Jesus. They sense His Presence. They seek to follow Him. Through faith in Christ they also learn to direct their prayers to the Father. That's a lot to keep up with at first!

The Holy Spirit, meanwhile, is quiet as a whisper. He resides so gently and unobtrusively inside that He is easily overlooked. As a consequence the Holy Spirit has been called the "mystery Person" of the Trinity. Why would God do things this way?

Our Disappearing Savior

I'm sure most of us have at one time or another thought that the disciples had it made. They had Jesus with them in the flesh! They could see Him, hear Him, touch Him, bring all of their questions and problems right to Him. What could be better? Actually, Jesus Himself said that it would be better for them that He was going away.[4]

> **Nevertheless, I tell you the truth: it is to your advantage that I go away, for if I do not go away, the Helper will not come to you. But if I go, I will send him to you.** John 16:7

Perhaps Jesus was talking about His upcoming death. He had to gain for them (and us) a "better resurrection."[5] Naturally, He had to "go away" to do that by dying on the cross. But He came back. Yes, but then He went away again and *stayed away*. This is apparently His idea of making it better for us!

Even poor doubting Thomas, who was allowed to have his faith strengthened by touching Jesus' wounds, was chided with the words that it would have been a great blessing for Him to have believed without seeing the Risen Christ in the flesh.[6] That includes all of us. We are evidently blessed by not seeing Jesus with our natural eyes. From the Lord's point of view gaining spiritual sight by means of faith is the greater blessing. That's where the Holy Spirit comes in.

Our Invisible Helper

If what we had really needed was the visible presence of Jesus with us always, then that is what God would have given us. But that is not what He did. Instead, He gives us "another Comforter" by placing the Holy Spirit right inside of us![7] Who could have guessed He would do that? Or that He could do it? Instead of a visible Savior, known for His sudden comings and goings, we have the indwelling presence of a steadfast, invisible Helper who never leaves us.

I suspect that all too often we focus on the invisible character of our indwelling Guest, rather than the amazing FACT of His steadfast presence. Would it help if I told you that it would truly bother you no end, if you could see Jesus all of the time? Of course there might be unlawful or immoral moments (God forbid) when you wouldn't want to be "forced" to encounter a visible Lord, or anyone else for that matter. Can you see, however, that even in some legitimate "private" moments, you wouldn't want the intrusion of God's visible presence? In our partly cleansed condition that would easily feel oppressive at times.

What is even harder to see is that we need "space" from God in order to freely choose to move closer to God. It's a free will issue. If Jesus reveals too much of Himself it "forces" our choice, either because we'd be drawn to Him like moths to a flame, or because fear (not love) would be making us act against our desires. He has to watch over that one for us. OK, that's as far as I'm going with this thought. The main idea is that with the Holy Spirit living permanently inside of us, we have the very comfortable knowledge of God's abiding presence without any uncomfortable sense of invasion of our privacy. How He pulls that off is still amazing to me!

What the Holy Spirit Does for Us

This is only meant to get you started. Discovering what the Holy Spirit has already been doing for you, is currently working on, and desires to do in the future should be more than enough to fill your days with the adventure of hosting such a helpful Guest.

1) Our Helper. Imagine anything you might need help with: memory, reason, skill; studying, planning, organizing; working, buying, trading; loving, laughing, weeping; cooking, cleaning, crafting… The list could be endless! All along He has been with us. He was there in the beginning helping us learn to nurse as babies, teaching us our native language, guiding us into play and laughter as little children.

Now the world's Greatest Teacher is living inside us. This can give us an edge in any field of endeavor: Learning how to yield ourselves to the Holy Spirit's enabling power can carry any of us much further than mere natural abilities alone. The key thing to remember is that *He is called the Helper, not the Doer.* It is still up to us to take the steps that He helps us with.

2) Our Sanctifier. That's a five dollar church word if ever there was one! Strictly speaking it means being set apart: We have been set apart as a dwelling place for God; we are now holy because He who lives in us is holy. In that sense we are already sanctified.[8]

But hold your horses! We're not in the home stretch yet. Between here and heaven, the Holy Spirit will be working to sanctify us step by step as He helps us separate from wrong thoughts, wrong beliefs, wrong attitudes, wrong actions and wrong desires.[9]

3) Our Truth Teller.[10] This is, perhaps, His most important and all-encompassing job. He has come to reveal truth to us so that we can a) recognize sin and turn from it, b) envision righteousness and turn towards it, and c) become ever more convinced that God's judgments in these matters is all that matters.[11]

Basically He points us to God's Word and to the Person of Jesus to awaken our conscience and settle the issue: Where the Bible is clear the case is closed; in other matters we look to Jesus. How would Jesus handle it? What would He do? What would He want us to do? Whatever is contrary to the nature and character of Jesus is sin; whatever aligns with Him is righteousness.

4) Our Guide. Not only does He show us truths to believe, He has also come to lead us in the true path. He is our Guide, our Companion in the way who knows the Way. If we are attentive to Him, He shows us the next right thing to do. In this way the one who is Truth can lead us step by step through each day and through the whole of our lives.

This carries His gift to us as Truth Teller into every dimension of life. By trusting our hearts to God through faith in Christ, the Holy Spirit lifts and leads us into a whole new way of living.[12] We emerge into the glorious liberty of the children of God![13]

5) Our Source of New Life. By dwelling within us the Holy Spirit is in position to help us dwell within Jesus. The indwelling Spirit is essential for our being able to experience, cultivate and live filled with the fruit of the Spirit—peace, love, joy, patience, kindness, goodness, faithfulness, gentleness, and self-control.[14] This good fruit comes to us as we abide in Christ through trusting and obeying His leadership over our lives. All of these beautiful and enjoyable qualities comprise that river of "living water" which Jesus said would flow out of our hearts.[15]

Naturally enough, the Holy Spirit is a self-starter. He isn't going to sit on His Hands waiting for us to get in the right mood in order to begin His divine assignments. With or without our permission He is ever at work helping us, sanctifying us, revealing truth to us, guiding us and supplying us with the fruit of new life. It just goes so much better when we cooperate! Good spiritual health is letting the Holy Spirit have His way.

Holy Spirit

CHAPTER 6

TRUE SPIRITUAL HEALTH

Spiritual healing goes deepest of all, deeper than healing of body or soul. And it is here—at this level of engagement—that the Holy Spirit brings incredible transformation. Even though the reality of our spirit lies beyond the ability of our five senses to experience, it nevertheless holds the answer to all that affects our lives. Every breakdown in heart, mind or body traces back to this deepest of all roots. God begins our spiritual healing through the gift of faith in Christ and the indwelling Spirit. However, there is one thing that necessarily depends upon us, before God can bring our spiritual life into genuine health.

Restore to me the joy of Thy salvation, and sustain me with a willing spirit. Psalms 51:12 NASB

The Deep Sickness

What is our deadliest sin-sickness? It is the turning of our innermost life from God to Self. In this we followed "our father" the devil who infamously declared his independence (and therefore rebellion) from God with a series of defiant "I wills": "I will ascend... I will sit on the throne... I will sit on the mount..."[1]

This deep sickness at the core of our being was inevitable, once sin broke our connection to God. No longer able to behold the Lord with sighted eyes, we lost the ability to carry His true Image within our hearts. Our hearts and minds have been veiled by the god of this world ever since.[2] Into this spiritual vacuum we inevitably began beholding ourselves! We became self-focused and self-centered.

The gospel has come to liberate us from our separation from God and restore the true image of our God "in the face of Jesus Christ."[3] By beholding Him we can grow ("be transformed") from glory to glory.[4] We are set free to live no longer for ourselves alone, but for Him who died for us.[5]

And he died for all, that those who live might no longer live for themselves but for him who for their sake died and was raised. 2 Corinthians 5:15

Until we are born again, we have no other option but to live with Self at the center. Now that Jesus has been revealed, we are given a daily choice: Will we seek and serve Him, or follow our own will into a life apart? The first healing of our spiritual disease, therefore, comes through the revelation of who Jesus is as our Lord and Savior. However, until Jesus becomes the Lord we freely choose to trust and follow each and every day, the healing of our spirit has not gone nearly far enough.

David prayed to be sustained a "willing spirit"—to fully be recovered from the sin that led him away from God and His ways.[6] That is true spiritual health! Like any other form of health it cannot be faked: Genuine surrender to and submission to the Lord Jesus will always produce His peace. Rebellion to His leadership or straying from His Person always robs us of peace. Having tasted the bitter fruit of going his own way, David yearned to stay yielded to and united to God.

As we gain spiritual health our questions inevitably change from self-centered, self-directed, self-promoting and self-defending to Jesus seeking: If we still ask "What do I want to do?" it is only to remind ourselves, "I know, I want to do what Jesus would want me to do!" As we allow Jesus to be our Lord, He is able to cleanse us of the spiritual and emotional garbage we carry inside. Then, as our inner life becomes cleansed and healed, we live in ever greater measures of freedom, peace and joy. This in turn becomes a wellspring of health to our bodies. That is truly being healed from the inside out.

Keep your heart with all vigilance, for from it flow the springs of life. Proverbs 4:22

A Spiritual Health Check List

Willingness is the coin of the realm when it comes to experiencing new life in the Spirit, genuine spiritual health and growth, as well as receiving guidance from the Lord. Have you ever seen someone trying to get a resistant dog on a leash to walk obediently in the direction the master wants to go—and at the pace the master desires to set? Some dogs are rebellious; some are easily distracted by cats or other dogs. Such dogs may not be taken out beyond necessity. Then there are other dogs who don't even need a leash, who go everywhere in tandem with their masters. That is our goal—to become so captivated by Jesus in our hearts that we no longer need the sometimes unpleasant discipline of being constrained by Him through our circumstances.

> **I will instruct you and teach you in the way which you shall go. I will counsel you with my eye on you. Don't be like the horse, or like the mule, which have no understanding, who are controlled by bit and bridle, or else they will not come near to you.** Psalm 32:8-9 WEB

If you would love to be readily and frequently guided, then the issue of living with a surrendered heart and a willing spirit is paramount. When Isaiah saw the Lord, he fully surrendered and became willing for anything.[7] So, let's review what a surrendered heart is saying to the Lord. Then keep checking your heart to make sure your surrender and willingness stay intact. Let the acronym SAAW remind you to look to Him.

S: Send whatever You desire to send.
Am I trusting the Lord with His free will?

A: Allow whatever You have to allow.
Am I trusting the Lord with His way of working with everyone else's free will, including my own? Including the enemy's?

A: Ask of me whatever You desire or require.
Am I fully willing to let the Lord take the lead?

W: Withhold me from and withhold from me whatever is necessary to fulfill Your plans.
Am I willing to wait upon the Lord to do things His way and in His time?

Beware: Even a twinge of unwillingness to surrender is a step towards the Great Rebellion. If you see it in you, you have met the enemy! Carry that thought captive to Christ.[8] True spiritual healing is a surrendered heart!

Don't think that the Enemy will let your desire to live surrendered to Jesus go unchallenged. You're going to have to learn the ways of spiritual warfare in order to stay free. We'll take a look at that in Chapter 9, but first let's walk through how to live a surrendered life—what the Bible calls "walking in the Spirit."

A Prayer of Surrender

Father, according to Your love and wisdom, send whatever You desire to send of Your grace and blessings, allow whatever You have to allow of free will and its consequences, ask of me whatever You desire or require of inward and outward obedience, withhold me from and withhold from me whatever is necessary to fulfill Your plans. Help me to fully trust that You are working in and through all things for my good and Your glory. Make me willing to be made willing to surrender everything to You that I may spend the better part of my days flowing in Your river of peace! May it carry me often into Your Presence and always into Your purposes.

CHAPTER 7

WALKING IN THE SPIRIT

The point of coming to Jesus to receive the life of grace is not to get free and then walk away. We are set free so that we can live in greater union with Jesus through His Spirit. The new creation life works best by 100% grace (God's part), 100% surrender (our part) and by 100% guidance (a cooperative adventure). We have all been guided by the Lord in many ways all of our lives—often by ways we were unable to recognize at the time. It enhances our daily walk with Jesus when we learn to recognize and cooperate with these un-self-conscious means of being guided by the Lord.

In order that the righteous requirement of the law might be fulfilled in us, who walk not according to the flesh but according to the Spirit.
Romans 8:4

God's Ways of Guiding Us

Our quest is to become so free that we can follow Jesus in everything! The truly healed and restored life is one that is continually given over to the Lord, seeking to walk with Him as He leads the way. For that we will need to learn what it means to be "walking in the Spirit" that He supplies.[1]

Let us begin by acknowledging that as great as His Word is—He even set it above His Name—God speaks to us in many more ways than scripture alone.[2] We are guided by His example (a visible word, however scripture displays Him), His voice (a spoken word, however we may receive it), and His Spirit (a living word, however He may inspire us).

It is easy to see from this that there is a progression of increasing intimacy from following the written Word of scripture to imitating Jesus' example to listening for His voice to yielding the whole flow of our daily life to His Spirit. Jesus gave us—His Bride on earth— more than a book when He pledged Himself to us as our Husband. He gave Himself to us![3]

Our new life in Christ comes through the forgiveness of our sins and through the gift of the indwelling Holy Spirit.[4] Just as Jesus died our death for us, so now He desires to live His life in us and through us. This happens beautifully whenever we yield ourselves to the Holy Spirit and walk in the steps He shows us. Whenever we are released to trust and obey, Jesus "comes to life" in us!

I have been crucified with Christ [in Him I have shared His crucifixion]; it is no longer I who live, but Christ (the Messiah) lives in me; and the life I now live in the body I live by faith in (by adherence to and reliance on and complete trust in) the Son of God, Who loved me and gave Himself up for me. Galatians 2:20 AMP

Walking in the Spirit has two distinct dimensions: conscious and unconscious. Though this may be a strange way of phrasing it, the truth is that we have been sleep walking with the Lord all of our lives. That is, He has been guiding us at countless times all along, but we may not have been consciously aware of the many specific ways by which He was leading us.

Our first task, therefore, is to identify and understand these hidden ways of un-self-conscious guidance. The Holy Spirit is like the perfect waiter who doesn't intrude upon our privacy by making His ways of serving us obvious. It is up to us to learn how to acknowledge Him so that He can more intimately and overtly direct our paths.

Lean on, trust in, and be confident in the Lord with all your heart and mind and do not rely on your own insight or understanding. In all your ways know, recognize, and acknowledge Him, and He will direct and make straight and plain your paths. Proverbs 3:5-6 AMP

Dimension One: Unselfconscious Guidance

Walking in the Spirit is like breathing which is hardly surprising since He is called the "breath of the Almighty" and He is the breath of life imparted to us both in creation and through the new birth.[5] This Spirit-empowered walk, therefore, is easy and natural—literally child's play!

In fact it was the Spirit, the great Teacher and Giver of life, who "secretly" taught us how to suckle, to eat, to speak, to walk, even to play. Every good thing about us including childhood is His gift to us, or will we have some "work" of our own apart from God to boast about? Not according to scripture, which says that we are saved by grace through faith and that not of ourselves, not of our works, "lest anyone should boast."[6]

Let us acknowledge then that this Spirit-empowered walk has been going on since birth as His gift to us. God said that even the "infancy" of Israel, the forty years of their wilderness journey, was a time when He "carried Israel" as a child: He led them through it all and then explained it to them later, so that they could understand and acknowledge what He had done.[7]

And in the wilderness, where you have seen how the Lord your God carried you, as a man carries his son, all the way that you went until you came to this place. Deuteronomy 1:31

Take a moment right now to look back over your life and see if you can recognize the Lord's past presence with you. Don't be "sheepish" about admitting the truth that the Holy Spirit has been speaking to you and showing you things all along. The truth is that if you haven't been listening to the Lord *at all*, you would undoubtedly be in an insane asylum, a prison, or a grave by now. To help jog your memory look over this check list of phrases. Not really understanding or appreciating the Holy Spirit's ways with us has created a vacuum which the public imagination filled with a kind of unwitting code language for describing the Spirit's operations. See if you can see the ways these phrases just might describe our Mystery Guest at work.

__A little bird whispered in my ear.
__I have a gut feeling this will work.
__It's just a hunch, but have you tried…
__Something just doesn't seem right about this.
__I've got a bad feeling about this.
__The thought just dropped in out of the blue!
__That same thought just occurred to me too!

__All of a sudden I remembered…
__This idea just stays on my mind…
__It's a feeling I just can't shake off.
__That gave me chills and goose bumps!
__What an incredible coincidence!

A Childlike Grace

To this day the greatest exemplars of what walking in the Spirit is like are little children. They do it wholly by "unself-conscious guidance."[8] Their sparkling qualities are His gift of grace to them and through them to us. Children are simply more open and trusting than we are, which makes them such splendid receivers of grace that they are masters at living in the Kingdom, showing us the way to go.[9]

But Jesus called them to him, saying, "Let the children come to me, and do not hinder them, for to such belongs the kingdom of God. Truly, I say to you, whoever does not receive the kingdom of God like a child shall not enter it." Luke 18:16-17

The Holy Spirit has been with us all along. He is always teaching us and leading us into life. He is the Giver and Sustainer of life.[10] Jesus told His disciples before the events of Easter and Pentecost that they already "knew" the Holy Spirit He would be sending, because the Spirit had been dwelling "with" them and would soon be "in" them.[11]

This same divine Person has been unceasingly with you in your journey, helping you, guiding you, teaching you and comforting you, even before you became a Christian, even from before birth![12]

Now the word of the Lord came to me, saying, "Before I formed you in the womb I knew you, and before you were born I consecrated you; I appointed you a prophet to the nations." Jeremiah 1:4-5

A Yielded Life

St. Augustine put it this way: "Love God and do as you please."[13] He means of course that once we "love God" by surrendering to

Him everything about our lives and loved ones and are willing to do His will above our own, then He begins to draw us by desires that please Him as well as ourselves.

Only fully yielded Christians can live the way Augustine recommends. However, even before we knew Him, God was already drawing us into doing many things that pleased us as well as Him. Examples of this are eating, sleeping, befriending, parenting, working, loving and laughing.[14] No one needs conscious guidance from the Lord to do good things which come to us with such natural grace attached.

> **[Not in your own strength] for it is God Who is all the while effectually at work in you [energizing and creating in you the power and desire], both to will and to work for His good pleasure and satisfaction and delight.** Philippians 2:13 AMP

Trusting is, therefore, essential to these everyday ways of Spirit-empowered guidance, since any interference by negative emotions disturbs the childlike manner of our walk. Proverbs calls us to acknowledge Him and trust Him, that He may "direct our paths."[15] Guidance happens naturally for trusting hearts as Hannah Whitall Smith explains in *The Christian's Secret of a Happy Life*.[16]

> *Above everything else trust Him... God cannot guide those souls who never trust Him enough to believe that He is doing it.*

The River of Peace

The river of peace is worth all the battles. There is a vision in Ezekiel of water flowing from the Temple that begins as a shallow stream and eventually becomes a river which no one can cross.[17] This gives us a picture of our life of faith flowing from the place of consecration and surrender, signified by the Temple and its Altar — the place where lives are offered in devotion to the Lord.

There is peace as we trust and obey, but at first it is all too easy to step out of the flow of His Spirit's gentle guidance. With practice we can learn to live in the peace Jesus supplies—a peace for our hearts (as we trust Him) and a peace for our "feet" (as we follow Him). The

Holy Spirit is a river of life to all who learn to live in Him and walk by Him.

For thus says the Lord: "Behold, I will extend peace to her like a river.
Isaiah 66:12

With practice, determined effort, childlike faith and tons of grace this flow of peace and divine purpose, which once was so hard to find (only ankle deep), will become a mighty river that lifts and carries you into great adventures in the Lord.

So what are you waiting for? Go ahead—jump in with both feet!

A Prayer for Discernment

Father, forgive me wherever I have thought or said that I have not heard Your voice or experienced Your guidance. I utterly renounce that false belief. The truth is that I am someone who knows how to be guided by You and who has been given ears to hear and eyes to see what You are speaking to me or showing me. I am learning how to listen for Your voice of wisdom through Your Word, through my inner life, and through other people. I am learning to recognize Your Hand—prompting, checking and guiding me. Thank You that You have been speaking to me and guiding me all of my life. Help me to recognize and acknowledge You in all of these ways, so that my eyes can open wider to give You credit and to more readily perceive Your ways of leading me.

CHAPTER 8

GUIDED BY THE SPIRIT

It's tremendously comforting to know that the lion's share of guidance in our lives is taking place without our even realizing it, whenever we trust the Lord enough to let His river of peace carry us through the day. We have walked by His Spirit even as kids. His Hands have always been steering us—to a degree—even at those times when our trust was shattered and His peace non-existent. But for goodness sake, let's don't stop with that. The next level of guidance is far more fun and adventurous. Learning to consciously seek specific guidance enables us to be carried into the dance of life with enhanced opportunities for intimacy with Jesus and for effectiveness in His service.

Therefore do not be foolish, but understand what the will of the Lord is. Ephesians 5:17

Dimension Two: Christ-Conscious Guidance

The Spirit-empowered walk described in the previous chapter is childlike and free. Not even being aware that it is happening is almost one of its requirements! On the other hand, the Spirit-led walk actually does require conscious and conscientious diligence and care in seeking it. It is harder work at first, but it is the way of the wise.[1]

The first principle of seeking this kind of "awake and aware" guidance is: "Don't ask, if you don't really want to know." The Lord is not out to satisfy our intellectual curiosity about His will. He prefers to lead us through our *obedience* to His will. The likelihood exists that He may not tell you what you want to hear, so be prepared to yield to His will and avoid the pitfall of poor King Ahab who didn't want his plans disturbed by a contrary word from the Lord.[2] As Hannah Whitall Smith advises, "An immediate obedience is the safest and easiest course."[3]

There are five "voices" that should harmonize: scripture, conscience, inward impressions, wise counsel and providential circumstances.[4] Tread softly in this arena—guidance is an art, not a science.

I. First Voice: Scripture

In His Word God provides boundaries and guidelines so that we can know right and wrong with clarity on many issues and see the general outline of a right path for our lives.[5] We, therefore, need to take the scriptures to heart so that the Holy Spirit may use them to direct us and keep us from error, just as we would study a map to navigate our way through dangerous and unfamiliar terrain.[6]

This guidance takes precedence over all else. Hence there is a real need to search the scriptures and keep things in balance. Some general guidelines to follow are "whatever is plainly taught must be obeyed"; "adhere to principles, not isolated texts"; and "keep the main thing, the main thing." The "main thing" is keeping love for Jesus and submission to Him as our first and foremost consideration.[7]

At times the Lord will even quicken His written Word, making it come alive with guidance about specific steps to take. Remember, though, that in Biblical times they didn't have airport searchlights. The lamp that lit their path on a dark night barely showed more than a few steps ahead at a time. He says His Word is like that kind of lamp.[8]

Rule of Thumb: Don't expect to hear a word spoken if it has already been written.

Negative Guidance: The Lord will never lead us contrary to His written Word.

Positive Guidance: General principles of scripture point the way and show the boundaries—but not all is made plain.

Consider this progression: *Good* is the wide range of what He permits by His Word; *better* is trying to find the path of His specific will for you; *best* is actually walking in the center of it.

II. Second Voice: Conscience

Though not infallible, "Do the next right thing" is a handy way of expressing that aspect of the Spirit-led walk which is a steady succession of right ideas to follow supplied by the Spirit to our minds. We are meant to cultivate wisdom and right understanding as one means of being guided by the Lord.[9]

We have been given the ability to make right judgments and are expected to use it: Common sense is a gift of God; its counterfeit is the natural mind. We have a duty to educate our consciences, renewing our minds by His Word.[10] At the same time we are told not to lean on our understanding at those times when we should be trusting.[11] How do you know if it is time to trust? Whenever something happens that you don't understand!

Curiously, it is not as hard to get wisdom as one might suppose. It's free for the asking, but the catch is you have to have a) the humility to realize you don't have wisdom and b) some basic confidence in His ability to send it your way.[12]

There are three "divine guides" that common sense and a reasonably renewed understanding can judge fairly easily:

1) Right Desire: Heart and feelings can safely be allowed to lead us if no moral law contradicts the direction they would take.

2) Obvious Necessity: Intellect and observation leave no room for doubt about the quick action that is needed in the moment.

3) Genuine Duty: The moral call is clear, even if it is undesired, and there is a sense that it would be dishonorable not to do it.

III. Third Voice: Inward Impressions

Movements of the Holy Spirit upon us, especially when we are at rest in the Lord, show us how to move in step with the Spirit.[13] Only the Lord can teach you this way of continual guidance.[14] Because leadings are often so faint, it really is a process of trial and error. But take heart, He loves it that we are seeking to be led and, after all, He is the best Teacher on earth.

For instance He instructs us to "walk humbly with our God."[15] Humility is not just the only appropriate posture; it actually positions us to receive the wisdom necessary for guidance.[16] Don't be too eager to proclaim that you've heard from the Lord, even if you have. Let events unfold by themselves. His wisdom will become evident to all.[17]

He speaks ever quieter, so we have to learn to become still, if we don't want to miss anything. Quieting our own interior landscape may seem daunting, but it truly is something that we can do.[18] Picture a pond surrounded by trees with the wind blowing and rain pelting the surface. A pebble tossed into it wouldn't be heard or noticed. Then see the pond on a totally calm day: The splash can be heard and every ripple followed to the shore. Now you be that pond and listen for His "pebbles"!

As with our own speech, both the Lord and the enemy have a message (thoughts or words) and an impression (tone of voice). Learn to recognize the ripple effect of their voice upon your soul. The enemy's voice often makes "a splash" that disrupts your inward sense of peace and well-being. The Lord's ripple effect is peace-filled.

Listen in quietness for the "still, small voice" and you will catch His gentle whispers.[19] Wait patiently upon Him. It is better to wait for the light to come than to proceed in the dark, but the moment you are sure, yield a complete obedience.

Rule of Thumb: When in doubt, wait it out; if you feel led, go ahead. Negative impressions (checking, grieving, restraining) caution us to stop, look and listen. Positive impressions (prompting, leading, impelling, calling) lead us forth.

Warning: Inward impressions may come from wrong spirits or from un-renewed areas of our souls (unhealed wounds, wrong desires, unmet needs, etc.). Proceed with caution!

The heart of the old nature is very deceptive.[20] Hannah Whitall Smith cautions, "It is not enough... for the leading to be very 'remarkable,' or the coincidences to be very striking, to stamp it as being surely from God."[21] Make sure that you stay submitted to the other means of guidance, especially matching up anything you think you hear with His Word. Inward impression can provide invaluable guidance, but they are also the most frequent culprits for leading people astray.

IV. Fourth Voice: Consensus of Wise Counsel

The counsel of others is not meant to be a substitute for one's own judgment, since every choice we face is an opportunity for the Lord to grow us in the proper use of the free will He has given us. God will use others to confirm, but rarely to give direction. Agreement of counselors may be a sign of God's leading. It needs to be heeded, but not followed slavishly.[22]

Who are the wise ones whose walk with the Lord you admire and who God has placed in your life? Make sure you seek them out—not people who will molly-coddle you.[23] Even so, keep in mind that His ultimate purpose is for us to be able to listen for ourselves. It is good to go to others for counsel, but we are not to lean on them—we are to learn to lean only on the Lord.[24]

V. Fifth Voice: Providential Circumstances

Reading providential signs is for confirmation only. Even open and closed doors are not a sign in themselves: Closed doors need to be respected, but they are not always of the Lord; neither are open doors. As a rule don't force your way past a closed door or turn from it in despair. Learn to wait upon the Lord to open what needs to be opened.[25] However, don't race through every open door you see—it could be a snare.

We are meant to let the Shepherd (not signs) go before us, leading us in the way. He is the way: *Sticking close to Him is the secret of guidance*.[26] We are also meant to mature to the point where we can hear and discern His voice. By Jesus' own description "lambs" may not hear His voice, but His "sheep"—those who have matured— certainly do.[27]

Slow Down Signs: Listen carefully at closed doors; pay attention to hindrances and disturbances "in the flow" of peace.

Proceed with Caution Signs: Open doors and coincidences usually indicate a right path; best of all is the river of joy and peace.

Guidance is different than obedience. With obedience it is "trust Him and do it" (the command is clear); with guidance it is "trust Him and try it" (the leading is uncertain). Guidance is the art of following a hunch and hunches are by nature experimental. Hold them lightly.

Above all, relax. Trying to be guided is like trying to be good. If you try too hard, you will foul it up by not trusting. Just as His goodness is already there for you to abide in, so is His guidance. Being overly self-conscious is disastrous in anything especially when graceful execution is required. Trust, trust, trust and row your spiritual boat gently down the stream.

A Prayer for Guidance

Father, now that you have given me "ears to hear and eyes to see," grant that I will become so sensitive to the Holy Spirit's promptings, checkings and leadings that I will practically be walking in His shoes. Help me learn to read all the signs Your Spirit is using to point the way forward for me. Let every part of me—body, soul and spirit—become a pathway for listening to Your call. Above all, keep me seeking to walk humbly with You, especially when it seems that I am getting a few things right. I trust Your love to watch over me, Jesus to liberate me (should I get snared), and the Holy Spirit to guide me. What an adventure this life can become—every step of the way!

CHAPTER 9

SPIRITUAL WARFARE

If only we could walk in the Spirit with our Lord in the Garden of Life. That would be heaven on earth. (It was once upon a time...) Instead we are plopped down here in the middle of a battlefield. Every square inch of the earth is contested territory—either the Lord is advancing his kingdom or the enemy is making gains. And there is no place more contested than those few inches within your breast—your heart. What's a poor, beleaguered (former) sinner to do? Take up spiritual arms and fight, that's what!

Therefore take up the whole armor of God, that you may be able to withstand in the evil day, and having done all, to stand firm.
Ephesians 6:13

The Battle for Your Heart

We have all been issued hearts the way recruits in boot camp have been issued rifles, but unless we learn how to keep them clean and well-guarded our hearts can become a weapon in the enemy's hand that is used against God, self and others. As we shall see there are two primary works of the Father that go on 24/7 for our conformation and transformation into a life like Jesus lived. However, the enemy has also read the Book, *knows this*, and has two very effective counter strategies. Engage the battle for your heart!

Our Number One Assignment

Our elementary spiritual warfare concerns the intense battle surrounding our daily life in Christ. Our job as soldiers is to make sure that our hearts stay surrendered to the Lord throughout the day—keeping us willing and able to trust and obey our Master and Commander (who is also our best Friend).[1] This is our number one assignment in life, given to us by Jesus Himself as the "first and great" commandment.[2]

45

Loving God with our whole heart certainly entails giving the whole of our life over to Him in full submission to His leadership. Such surrender and centering of our life in Him is not possible without the gift of faith; living un-surrendered and un-centered in Him is unthinkable once true faith has come. Indeed a living faith always carries us into this position of humble, trusting dependence and willingness to follow the One who has revealed such love to us.[3]

Our hearts are either moving towards surrender or drifting into the Great Rebellion. This not Star Trek: There is no Neutral Zone. There are only two spiritual principles at work in our universe and they are *always* at work upon us. This is why the keeping of the first commandment is so critical to our life mission: We cannot fulfill our secondary purpose in the lives of others if we do not learn to stay united to His life (our primary purpose).

The level of peace and confidence we have in God will declare the issue all day long. That's God's way of giving us feedback moment by moment on how well we are doing with the most important thing we need to be doing—trusting and obeying Him.[4] This is the battle for one's own life and it is waged in the heart.[5]

In boot camp all new recruits are issued rifles and taught to protect their lives and the lives of their comrades. In the battle of daily life our rifle is our heart. The enemy wants to get his finger on the trigger of our heart and start firing it off at ourselves and others. Such misfires are almost irresistible when we don't keep our heart clean and clear. On the other hand, suppose that your heart is under the Lord's control. Then He can use you to give mercy, peace and patience where it is needed as you go through your day. That's much better isn't it? Our heart is a powerful weapon for advancing either the kingdom of God or the kingdom of darkness.

Trusting His Hands; Seeking His Face

Here is another principle of simplicity that companions with trust and obey: No matter what the enemy is doing, God is also at work to accomplish His good purposes. This is especially true of the dual dynamics of conformation and transformation. Since the great battle of daily life is for our heart, we need to trust His Hands and seek His

Face. In this way we will grow even as we may groan under the weight of unwanted attacks and difficult circumstances.

1) His Hands: God is at work on all things in our lives with one great purpose in mind. We need to know, understand and be in agreement with that purpose, or our lives will not make sense, nor will we realize the focal point of the enemy's attacks. God's Hands are always at work to conform you to Christ—shaping you from the outside in.

Picture the Lord reaching through all of the outward circumstances of your life, seeking to center you on the Potter's Wheel.[6] What is His goal in each and every moment? To draw out of you a Christ like response, or (if you can't yet do that) to prepare you to be able to respond as the new creation you are at some point down the road. The ultimate good that God has in mind is not just His blessings being poured into our lives, but the incomparable blessing of actually becoming more like Jesus in this life.

> **And we know that for those who love God all things work together for good, for those who are called according to his purpose. For those whom he foreknew he also predestined to be conformed to the image of his Son.** Romans 8:28-29

2) His Face: What is God's work on our interior? His primary purpose is to transform us into the Image of His Son from the inside out—by revealing His Image to us. The Father reveals the Son; the Son reveals the Father.[7] Whenever we get our spiritual eyes back on Jesus, we experience a shift from being self-centered to being Christ-centered.

This interior transformation happens as we "see" by faith some offering of grace in Jesus that enables us to fully surrender to whatever He has allowed or is asking of us. Once we again become centered and surrendered, submitted and committed, the good fruit of His Spirit flows into us and through us. In this way His Face transforms us into His Image.[8]

But we all, with unveiled face beholding as in a mirror the glory of the Lord, are transformed into the same image from glory to glory, even as from the Lord, the Spirit. 2 Corinthians 3:18 WEB

These two great works of God—conformation and transformation—are going on all of the time. Always the Father's Hands are upon us to raise up whatever we surrender to Him and to work through all things to increase our willingness to surrender all, even if we are fighting against what He is doing through our ignorance of His ways. At the same time the revelation of Jesus Christ is working within us at all times, however little we may be aware of it, to transform the way that we live and to enable us to surrender to the Father.

This process can be greatly enhanced by our cooperation. We can make it our goal to more frequently choose to surrender to the work of His Hands; we can also choose to more actively seek His Face and re-surrender at any moment. As you learn this you will discover that you are in the driver's seat where your spiritual growth is concerned! You will have mastered this vital tactic of our elementary spiritual warfare.

Let's see how this plays out. The Father has His Hands on our lives like a Master Potter working with absolutely everything (the good, the bad and the seemingly indifferent) to accomplish His great desire—to refashion us into children who display the nature of His Son. As a potter exerts great pressure with his hands to center clay on the wheel, the Father also works through the stress in our lives to bring us again and again to the place of inward surrender.

Like un-centered clay we often try to fly off the wheel! But under the pressure ("humble yourselves under the mighty hand...")[9] we finally stretch our faith vision to see something in the Lord that helps us to yield our stubborn resistance and say, "Not my will, but Yours be done."

The work of His Hands helps us to seek His Face! From this hallowed place of surrender the Father is able to raise us into new life—just as a potter raises the centered clay into the form he envisions.

Going through Our Day like Jesus

Since the Father is working 24/7 to conform us to Christ, it will certainly help us to cooperate with Him if we gain vision for what that process looks like. Though outward works are important fruit to cultivate, for the purpose of this chapter, let's consider what it means to be conformed to Christ in terms of the inner life and your emotional state.[10]

Would you like to go through your days the way Jesus did? No one alive has walked through daily life with more love, more peace, or more joy. Yet no one alive has ever had a tougher assignment to carry out or faced more opposition. Consider how your approach to daily life might change if you would follow Jesus in these ways:

1) Love and joy: Jesus was able to keep joy and love alive in His Heart because He was masterful at forgiving sinful people. Would you like to go through your day free of hurt and offense like Jesus did? You have Him inside of you to help you forgive. The freedom of living with a truly forgiving heart is well worth all the effort.

2) Acceptance: Jesus suffered rejection by many people He deeply loved, yet He was able to live with His Heart secure, knowing He was loved by the One who matters most. Would you like to go through your day protected and filled by God's love for you like Jesus did? You have the same Father devoted to you. Value His acceptance of you above the opinions of others and you will work your way through to a faith that knows the joy of an established heart.

3) Peace and guidance: Jesus was able to live in complete dependence upon God's control of the world, not His, and yet He was peace-filled all of the time, no matter what the enemy was stirring up, because He kept trusting the Father with all things and was willing to obey in all things. Would you like to go through your day with peace and trust like Jesus did? You have a new nature in you that loves to live His way of trust and obedience. Reach deep and go for the gold by stepping out beyond your comfort zone every time the Spirit beckons.

4) Stress free: Jesus saw people all around Him carrying heavy burdens and living with great anguish and injustice, but He never got burned out, over-burdened, angry or depressed in serving God. Would you like to be able to care for others in your daily life like Jesus did? He is right beside you, willing to help you learn how to let Him carry your burdens.

This is the way of life that Jesus wants to live in us by His Spirit, and our Father is so zealous for giving it to us that He is making all things serve this higher purpose. What's to stop us?

The Counter Feints of the Enemy

Certainly the enemy cannot stop this work of the Father's Hands —he is a defeated foe! Furthermore, God hates every evil and has determined and declared that all things will be made to work for the good of the people He is redeeming.

Meditate on this life-changing truth: The enemy cannot make the evil he does through human sin stick to anyone. God will overturn it all and make even the worst things the enemy does work for our good. So how does the enemy make evil stick? By getting us to bind the hurt, pain and injustice of the past to ourselves through bitterness of heart and by unbelief in God's promises. We are being manipulated into becoming our own captors! This is monstrous, outrageous and infernally ingenious all at the same time. Don't fall for it a moment longer!

If God is working upon us through all things by His Hands and working within us through all things by His Spirit to conform us to Christ, then the enemy (having read the Bible) is also working through everything to oppose God's work...

1) By tempting us to doubt that all things are working for our good (thus trying to counter the work of His Hands) and...

2) By "drawing us away" from the revelation of Jesus Christ (thus trying to counter the work of His Face).[11] As Jack Deere once said, "The enemy has W.M.D.'s of his own—Weapons of Mass Distraction"—that are designed to shift our focus away from the Lord.[12]

Once we are no longer beholding our matchless God with a heart of confident faith, we are prey to the enemy and of little threat to his kingdom. Even worse, we are unwittingly being re-shaped into the image of the ultimate fallen one, Satan, who is the most unforgiving and anxious being in the universe.

Have you been tempted to doubt the work of God's Hands? Have you been distracted from keeping your focus on Jesus? Then be prepared to fight! You get to choose what you want to believe and whose image you want to focus on and live by. If something *in you* doesn't want to trust in, surrender to and rely upon your God you have just met the enemy's handiwork—Self! Don't let it reign over you. Carry it captive to Christ instead.

Like those who rebuilt the walls of Jerusalem, we have to learn to do the work of the Kingdom with our sword and shield at our side, if we want to see the old stronghold walls of self-protection come down and the new, glorious walls of His salvation go up.[13] How long will that campaign take? Only He knows. But we can be sure of this: It will be well worth the effort it takes to fully enter His Kingdom in this life. Fight the good fight of faith!

> **I have fought the good fight, I have finished the race, I have kept the faith. Henceforth there is laid up for me the crown of righteousness, which the Lord, the righteous judge, will award to me on that Day, and not only to me but also to all who have loved his appearing.**
> 2 Timothy 4:7-8

A Prayer for a Warrior's Heart

Father, thank You for all of the ways that You are training me for those conflicts with the enemy that cannot be avoided. May I ever trust that You are also fighting with me and for me. I fully accept this calling upon my life—to fight the good fight of faith—and I realize that the first battle is always for my own heart—in order to keep it surrendered to You. Make me willing to be made willing to surrender everything to You, each and every day. I want to keep loving Jesus and walking in His Spirit!

CHAPTER 10

THE BAPTISM OF POWER

Jesus actually told the first disciples "Don't leave home without this!"
So important is this spiritual empowerment that even the followers who had
been trained by Him in person, who had received saving faith and the
indwelling Spirit on Easter evening, even these dedicated believers were
told to stay in Jerusalem and pray to be "baptized with the Holy Spirit."[1] If
they needed it, don't we?

"And behold, I am sending the promise of my Father upon you. But
stay in the city until you are clothed with power from on high."
Luke 24:49

Will You Ask for This?

Unlike the gift of the indwelling presence of the Holy Spirit, this baptism of power is not automatic, involuntary or unheralded. You have to desire it and ask for it, sometimes praying and waiting diligently for it to come. On the other hand, it can just as easily show up with the first prayer uttered, but rarely does this empowerment come upon a person who isn't looking for it. That's how it was with the first disciples: They were told by Jesus to seek it through prayer. Why would we think it would be any different for us?

Why would anyone not go for this? I hope you never find out! Oh, you may one day say, as I and countless others could, that it was this or that fear or offense which hindered us *in the beginning*. But if you press in to receive it (as I hope you will) then there is that unidentifiable gift of grace within you carrying you past the many obstacles to receiving this blessing. In this regard it is similar to receiving salvation. There are plenty of obstacles in everyone's life turning them from the way of faith, but once you have been saved, you really can't imagine anyone refusing the offer.

The Surpassing Power

It is impossible to read the gospels and not be surprised and delighted by the supernatural events that seem so natural wherever Jesus goes. Miracles were happening around Him with breath-taking frequency. On at least two separate occasions He even sent His disciples out and they took part in it too. Just for the record, none of them had ever been to seminary or were previously trained as prophets or priests. They were regular people like you and me.[2] It clearly surprised and delighted them that they were able to do many of the supernatural things that Jesus did, such as healing all manner of diseases and casting out demons.[3]

Where these supernatural events only meant to happen through Jesus' earthly ministry? Evidently not! After His resurrection, Jesus carefully instructed His recently born-again disciples to wait for what He called "the promise of my Father." They were to stay in Jerusalem until they could be "clothed with power from on high."[4] Did they just hang out, hoping it would show up? No, they sought it diligently, praying for it to come to them. Once it arrived, the supernatural flow of miracles broke forth all over again, along with extreme boldness in witnessing. The Book of Acts chronicles the way that this original band of regular folks became strong in the Word of the Lord and in deeds of power by the Holy Spirit.

Were these supernatural events only meant to happen through the ministry of the apostles? Definitely not! The Early Church for the first two centuries was characterized by miracles and deeds of power. These continued in sporadic outbreaks throughout the next 18 centuries, often through uniquely gifted individuals, rather than trained clergy. In fact healing miracles and supernatural deeds have always been one of the primary qualifications for bestowing the designation of "sainthood" by the Roman Catholic Church. The RC's are not alone in this. Periods of revival, seasons of persecution, the birthing of new movements have also witnessed the supernatural workings of God through devoted individuals.

Since the Pentecostal/Charismatic movement began in the early 1900s, however, millions of people have been moving in the supernatural operations of the Holy Spirit for miracles, healings and demonic deliverance. "Birthing" the revelation of the baptism of power back into the church was both joy and battle for those early Pentecostals. Ironically, the movement was born in a stable at Azusa Street in Los Angeles, California (sound familiar?).[5] For years it struggled to survive outside the camp due to the entrenched ridicule and hostility of the mainline denominations which rejected the truth of the revelation they had received. Now, it is the largest and fasted growing branch of Christianity in the world. You can be a part of it, too.

Why Don't We Get this Automatically?

Why didn't we get the baptism of power in the starter kit God gave us when we became born again?[6] That's a fair question. No explanation is given, though there are two kinds of facts which show us that it usually comes later: Biblical facts and the personal experience of Christians. The Biblical fact is that it came later for the disciples. They were born again in the Upper Room on the evening of the Resurrection and received the indwelling Spirit at that time. The baptism of power came 50 days later on the day of Pentecost, after praying and waiting for it as Jesus directed.

The early Pentecostal pioneers at the end of the 19th century were deliberately seeking this experience to be restored to the church. Ever since then, the majority of Christians who have received it, experienced it as coming *after* their salvation experience, not concurrent with it. For this reason it has often been called the "second blessing," though in reality there are no limits to the revelatory experiences Christians can have. These facts show us that it often comes later, but they don't tell us why.

Perhaps, although this is mere supposition, the Lord has intended for it to be separate in order that the beauty and power of the baptism in the Spirit would not overshadow the beauty and power of having the Holy Spirit dwelling secretly and silently within us. The indwelling presence of the Holy Spirit is united to us—it doesn't come and go as the manifestation of the Holy Spirit does when the gifts of power are in operation. It is certainly good for us to know that salvation and the indwelling Spirit go hand in hand. That way our salvation-confidence can be based upon our faith in

55

what the unchanging Word of God says that Christ has done for us, regardless of our feelings.

With the baptism of the Spirit feeling and experience rise to the forefront. Moving in the power gifts requires attentiveness to the manifest presence of the Holy Spirit. The anointing of His presence comes and goes like the wind, and so does our sense of His leading or directions. That's no foundation for confidence about our eternal position in Christ. From this standpoint it is an extremely good thing that our salvation doesn't depend upon sensing the Holy Spirit, but in believing God's Word alone.

What Comes with It?

These are observations based on general experience, so there are plenty of exceptions in real life. This is just to get you started in recognizing some of the benefits of this experiential encounter with the Holy Spirit. The best way to find out what the baptism in the Spirit is all about is to seek it wholeheartedly and then, when it comes your way, you will be able to explore it from the inside, not the outside.

1) A greater sensitivity to the Holy Spirit. Many Christians (not all) who only have the indwelling Spirit display very little practical awareness of the Holy Spirit's day to day operations in their lives. For them the Holy Spirit is indeed the "Mystery Person" of the Trinity. This is never the case for believers who have received the baptism of power. Not only do they know that they have met the Holy Spirit, they have a graced ability from that encounter to connect the dots of personal experience and recognize the Holy Spirit's presence and activity in all kinds of ways that they had previously attributed to other causes.

2) A greater ability to comprehend the scriptures. Unquestionably, there have always been pastors and teachers who could understand and communicate the Word of God, regardless of whether or not they received the baptism of power. Nevertheless, for the vast majority of Christians the Bible is a difficult book to penetrate and comprehend. Those who have been baptized in the Holy Spirit, however, universally report that they now have a much greater ability to read the scriptures and receive revelation directly from them. The answer to this riddle is easy: The Holy Spirit who wrote the scriptures is, in some significant way, more personally known and accessible to them.

3) A greater ability to engage in spiritual warfare. The discerning of spirits is one of the nine manifestation gifts of the Spirit.[7] Not everyone who is baptized in the Holy Spirit, becomes a vessel for the full manifestation of this gift to operate, just as not all Christians are gifted at evangelism, but every Christian can share their faith. Similarly, few Spirit baptized believers see into the invisible realms, but most of them typically display a greater sensitivity to the presence of evil spirits as well as the Holy Spirit. They are willingly trained as spiritual warriors for intercession or for demonic deliverance. This does not guarantee the accuracy of their discernment, anymore than having sight guarantees you won't walk into a door jamb or slip stepping off a curb. But it does give you a practical advantage over an unsighted person.

4) A greater potential for being led by the Spirit. An enhanced ability comes with the empowerment to sense the leading, prompting, checking and grieving of the Holy Spirit. This does not mean that all individuals choose to submit to these overtures, but for those who do, a heightened awareness of and sensitivity to the Holy Spirit is indispensable for being guided by the Lord step by step through the day. Just look at the way Paul was guided by the Holy Spirit. Certainly, he put a lot of stock in the Word of God, but he followed the path the Holy Spirit led him by within boundaries set by the Word. Jesus didn't give us only a Book to follow; He gave us His Holy Spirit to lead us as well.

5) A greater ability to pray for healings and miracles. Without doubt God hears every prayer and heals people at times in all denominations and churches. Unquestionably, His sovereign will is inscrutable. Every one of us experiences perplexing, heart-breaking times when prayers go unanswered. No one bats 100%. Even 5% would be a great average where dramatic, immediate answers to prayer for healing is concerned. Having said this, it is nevertheless a fact of history that Pentecostalism was birthed—just like the Early Church was birthed—through vast occurrences of supernatural power for healings and deliverances. And it continues to this day.

If you want to see tremendous miracles and multitudes of healings you may have to travel to the Third World, but you will only find it being done there through Holy Spirit baptized and empowered individuals and churches. As a general rule, only Spirit baptized believers move in the manifestation or "power" gifts of the Holy Spirit: prophecy, wisdom, knowledge, discerning spirits, miracles, healing, faith, tongues and interpretation of tongues. Though these gifts have some counterparts in ordinary Christian life, as supernatural manifestations they have a unique character all their own.

6) A greater boldness for spreading the gospel. Because of the qualities listed above and because of the enabling power of the Holy Spirit baptism, there is often more boldness and success in spreading the gospel—just as Jesus said there would be. Remember that His specific purpose in having his born again disciples pray for the "empowerment from on high" was for the purpose of world evangelism. Do not think of this simply as sharing faith and preaching the Word. The truly powerful combination then, as now, is signs and wonders (healings and miracles) *accompanying* the Word.[8]

What Doesn't Come?

Maturity and true Christian character cannot be conveyed to us by any gift. They must be cultivated over time. The baptism of power is made available to empower us for witnessing to the Risen Christ, for deeds of power, and by enhancing our life in Christ with greater conscious connection to the Holy Spirit. Character and integrity are cultivated in us by the indwelling presence of the Holy Spirit—if we are attentive to His work in us. By convicting, convincing, and judging us where sin and righteousness are concerned, the Holy Spirit cleanses us of our old ways and enables us to live as new creations.

The indwelling Spirit is essential for our being able to experience, cultivate and live filled with the fruit of the Spirit—peace, love, joy, patience, kindness, goodness, faithfulness, gentleness, and self-control. It is He who lifts us into new life and then flows through us, carrying us with peace and freedom from one moment to the next whenever we are released by faith-surrender to Jesus. You don't need to be baptized with power to experience this or excel at this. That's not what the baptism is about, though it certainly should bring enhancements to our ability to abide in Christ and live by the Spirit.

Sadly, many who have been baptized in the Spirit fail to cultivate the fruit of the Spirit in their lives. Please, guard against this. The baptism of power does not guarantee spiritual growth. It is not a short cut to maturity, the fruit of the Spirit, real holiness, integrity or character. You can be baptized in the Spirit and display none of these essential elements of a faithful believer. Don't let that be you! The truth is that with the proper combination of these two gifts any believer can become a valiant warrior who advances the Kingdom. Jesus knew the risks and still He commanded His disciples to pray and seek this empowerment "from on high." Why not take Him up on the offer?

A Prayer to be Baptized in the Holy Spirit

Lord Jesus, I want everything You have for me! I don't care what others might say or think: I only care about You and what You desire to do in my life. Just as it says in Your Word, I am now asking for you to baptize me in the Holy Spirit. Help me set aside any fears or doubts I might have, and open wide to receive this "power from on high" which You alone pour out upon Your believing people. I declare to You this day that I am willing to receive the gift of tongues and any of the nine gifts of power that You would choose to give me. May I always be willing to use them, not for my own advancement, but for Your glory and the good of Your people. Help me persevere in prayer and expectancy until the Holy Spirit comes upon me with power.

Holy Spirit

CHAPTER 11

PRAYING IN TONGUES

Do you have to? No, but you can if you want to and you just may want to. Paul did. In fact he was glad that he prayed in tongues more than the people to whom his letters were addressed. Since he also wrote more of the New Testament than anyone else, he ought to know why something this scandalous is so secretly good!

I thank God that I speak in tongues more than all of you.
1 Corinthians 14:18

How It Began

It is worth remembering that the gift of tongues came as a complete surprise. No one in the Upper Room was seeking tongues: *They were all seeking power.* Just ten days earlier they had been commanded by Jesus to stay in Jerusalem and pray for "power from on high" that would help them spread the good news of His resurrection and do the supernatural works He had done.[1] Apparently Jesus didn't consider that being born again and receiving the indwelling Spirit (from Him personally!) was sufficient for completing anyone's assignment under the New Covenant. So there they were, "gathered in one place" in prayer and expectancy for the arrival of something Jesus wanted them to have.

What came was the "the baptism of the Holy Spirit." The first outward sign of this empowering experience was the sound of a "mighty rushing wind"; next came "divided tongues as of fire" resting above each one; then came what we call the private prayer language. These devoted men and women had begun by praying in their native language, but when the baptism of the Spirit occurred their prayers and praises shifted into languages they had never spoken before.[2] Since there was no need for an interpretation—this was a private meeting of disciples—they simply praised God with these new languages out of the abundance of emotion welling up within them, evidently trusting the Lord to understand the content of their speech.[3]

> Then the day of Pentecost arrived, they were all together in one place. And suddenly there came from heaven a sound like a mighty rushing wind, and it filled the entire house where they were sitting. And divided tongues as of fire appeared to them and rested on each one of them. And they were all filled with the Holy Spirit and began to speak in other tongues as the Spirit gave them utterance. Acts 2:1-4

What then ensued was offense and controversy. It has surrounded and hounded the practice of tongues ever since. The exuberant, exhilarated, ecstatic gathering got noisy! On festival days Jerusalem was packed with people from all over the Mediterranean basin. It didn't take long to draw a multitude of "amazed and astonished" onlookers. No doubt some sensed the spiritual nature of what was taking place; others mocked, deriding them for being drunk on "new wine." That was a very interesting observation in light of Jesus' comparison of His ministry to new wine, but it wasn't intended as a compliment to either Jesus or His disciples.[4] When confronted with strange and bewildering occurrences some are intrigued; others are frightened. This division continues into our own day.

> Now there were dwelling in Jerusalem Jews, devout men from every nation under heaven. And at this sound the multitude came together, and they were bewildered, because each one was hearing them speak in his own language. And they were amazed and astonished, saying, "Are not all these who are speaking Galileans? And how is it that we hear, each of us in his own native language? ...we hear them telling in our own tongues the mighty works of God." And all were amazed and perplexed, saying to one another, "What does this mean?" But others mocking said, "They are filled with new wine." Acts 2:5-8, 11-13

Peter took good advantage of the situation and steered the people's attention to the Hebrew Scripture prophecy where power such as this was promised to be given in the "latter days" — days which had now arrived along with the astounding signs. Peter spoke to shift their focus from the sign which was offending them to the salvation Jesus offers and the baptism of power they, too, could receive. He was the first, but certainly not the last, Pentecostal preacher to try to get people to look past the offense of tongues to see the gift in a wider, more inviting, context. Following in his footsteps, we now turn to examine the private prayer language in the wider context of many scriptures.

Is It Necessary?

Tongues are not necessary for getting anyone to heaven. For that you must be born again through faith alone in Christ alone.[5] If that is all you are looking for, then you needn't look any further. But Jesus would want you to. Remember, it was the Lord who commanded His first believers to seek the baptism of power. When they received it, tongues came with it. Are tongues, therefore, necessary for receiving the baptism in the Spirit? That's putting the question the wrong way around. Tongues are a sign that the baptism in the Spirit has been received. It certainly operated in that way for the leaders of the Early Church who expected this sign to come forth when they prayed for the Spirit baptism.

Peter saw the sign of tongues falling on Cornelius' household as he preached to them which indicated to him that they had received the Holy Spirit. In this incident faith-conversion and Spirit baptism occurred at the same time. Peter also learned from this experience that water baptism doesn't have to come first.

While Peter was still saying these things, the Holy Spirit fell on all who heard the word. And the believers from among the circumcised who had come with Peter were amazed, because the gift of the Holy Spirit was poured out even on the Gentiles. For they were hearing them speaking in tongues and extolling God. Then Peter declared, "Can anyone withhold water for baptizing these people, who have received the Holy Spirit just as we have?" And he commanded them to be baptized in the name of Jesus Christ. Then they asked him to remain for some days. Acts 10:44-48

When Paul came across twelve believers in Greece who had not "received the Holy Spirit," he prayed for them and they began speaking in tongues. This was evidence enough that they had received the same baptism of power as the disciples at Pentecost.

> And he said to them, "Did you receive the Holy Spirit when you believed?" And they said, "No, we have not even heard that there is a Holy Spirit." ...On hearing this, they were baptized in the name of the Lord Jesus. And when Paul had laid his hands on them, the Holy Spirit came on them, and they began speaking in tongues and prophesying. Acts 19:2, 5-6

Even the unbelieving magician, Simon, "saw" the sign as evidence that power from the Holy Spirit had been received.

> Then they laid their hands on them and they received the Holy Spirit. Now when Simon saw that the Spirit was given through the laying on of the apostles' hands, he offered them money, saying, "Give me this power also, so that anyone on whom I lay my hands may receive the Holy Spirit." Acts 8:17-19

In light of these passages we can see that the gift of tongues, or the private prayer language, and the baptism of the Spirit go together. We can't say that it's impossible to be baptized in the Holy Spirit without speaking in tongues (for nothing is impossible with God). But we can say it would be an unusual breach of the Biblical pattern: Tongues are *the* sign that the baptism of power has been received. We can also say from this that if you want to pursue the supernatural workings of Holy Spirit, you will need to be open to receiving the prayer language. It is not for us to dictate to the Lord how He should empower us!

What's It For?

Tongues would be interesting enough if they were "merely" a sign of the mighty power which comes with the baptism in the Spirit. It is a gateway, therefore, leading to the nine gifts of power coming up in a later chapter.[6] However, the private prayer language is more than a sign or a gateway to better things: It carries powers of its own.

Prayer in tongues "builds up" the believer. The private prayer language is always available to us for praying or singing, either silently or aloud. This strengthens us in our inner spirit.

But you, beloved, build yourselves up in your most holy faith; pray in the Holy Spirit. Jude 20

The one who speaks in a tongue builds up himself, but the one who prophesies builds up the church. 1 Corinthians 14:4

Speaking with tongues and deliverance are signs that go with believing. Christians who speak in tongues also exhibit boldness and willingness to do the work of demonic deliverance.

And these signs will accompany those who believe: in my name they will cast out demons; they will speak in new tongues. Mark 16:17

Praying in tongues is a way of thanking, praising and glorifying God.

For they heard them talking in [unknown] tongues (languages) and extolling and magnifying God. Acts 10:46 AMP

What am I to do? I will pray with my spirit, but I will pray with my mind also; I will sing praise with my spirit, but I will sing with my mind also. 1 Corinthians 14:15-16

Praying in tongues is a way of interceding for others. This is especially helpful when we don't know what to pray for, or when we want to keep on praying but are feeling hindered by saying the same thing over and over again.

Praying at all times in the Spirit, with all prayer and supplication. To that end keep alert with all perseverance, making supplication for all the saints. Ephesians 6:18

Praying in tongues provides direct access between our spirit and God's Spirit. It releases the deep burdens within our hearts, cares and concerns that we may only dimly comprehend. Not only that, but by praying in tongues, we literally give the Holy Spirit an opportunity to use our own tongue to intercede through us!

Likewise the Spirit helps us in our weakness. For we do not know what to pray for as we ought, but the Spirit himself intercedes for us

with groanings too deep for words. And he who searches hearts knows what is the mind of the Spirit, because the Spirit intercedes for the saints according to the will of God. Romans 8:26-27

Paul desired that every believer would speak in tongues—as well as prophesy.

Now I want you all to speak in tongues, but even more to prophesy.
1 Corinthians 14:5

Desire to receive and cultivate your own prayer language. Then perhaps prayer in tongues in public and prophecy will come as additional gifts.

Therefore, one who speaks in a tongue should pray for the power to interpret... For you may be giving thanks well enough, but the other person is not being built up. 1 Corinthians 14:13, 17

CHAPTER 12

THE ETIQUETTE OF INTIMACY

The lessons we receive through the School of the Spirit are actually disciplines intended to correct us, by pruning away our old fallen ways. At times that instruction will seem blunt, even impersonal, as the Holy Spirit uses adverse circumstances to mold and re-shape us. Additionally, the point of the lesson is something clearly defined in scripture—a virtue required of us that is unarguable. In this final chapter we will seek to lift the veil on aspects of our relationship with the Holy Spirit that are more intimate and subtle and, therefore, harder to describe. That should not surprise us. The closer we get to any mystery, the more mysterious it becomes.

To them God chose to make known how great among the Gentiles are the riches of the glory of this mystery, which is Christ in you, the hope of glory. Colossians 1:27

A Good Pair of Shoes

One of the first things everyone notices about the indwelling presence of the Holy Spirit is that He doesn't seem to be there! Oh, we sense well enough when He *seems* to be absent, and we certainly are aware when He is manifesting His presence—may we have more of those times *please*. But, if we are honest about it, much of the time He can be easily forgotten or overlooked. He fits into us so well that, like a good pair of shoes, you don't even notice Him at all. That may sound like a shockingly casual way of talking about the Living God—He is far from being a mere footwear—nevertheless, this whole new way of living in us is His desire.

We are to "walk in Him" just as we would a pair of shoes that is both comfortable and protective.[1] He loves us far too much to want to be the kind of spooky, super-serious, uncomfortable presence that would have us jumping out of our shoes at every turn. Nor would that serve His purpose. He doesn't intend to draw attention to Himself, but to Jesus. So, naturally, He is not forever saying to us,

"Here I am! How'd you like what I just did? What do you think about that idea I gave you?"

It is not necessary, therefore, to anxiously apologize for not noticing Him, or thinking of Him. Simply thank Him whenever the reminder comes that your mind has drifted away from God and Jesus and refocus. Of course you're not going to notice the Holy Spirit (most of the time). That's the whole point! We can get so super-serious around the subject of God that we may miss the great good fun He has in doing things for us on the sly. Don't you love doing things secretly for your loved ones? Their joy is your reward. So too with Holy Spirit.

Becoming One

If we could bludgeon the English a bit, we would say that the goal of the Atonement is *at-one-ment*. Just as Jesus is in the Father and the Father is in Jesus, so Jesus wants to be in us and have us be in Him.[2] The way this is done is through the Holy Spirit becoming *at-one* with us. This cannot be forced, nor does it need to be. Grace works best as we seem to do nothing but trust.

Consider how it would be if you were trying to be *at-one* with your body. At the most fundament level you and your body are already seamlessly joined, how and where you don't know. You just take it for granted and go about your day. We don't go through our days intensely aware of our body, unless something is wrong with it. Otherwise, it is there, powerfully enabling us by sense and exertion to enter into the world surrounding us and partake of its life.

So, too, we are sealed by the Holy Spirit—united to Him in our spirit at the deepest level of our soul, beyond sight, beyond comprehension. Don't try to go through your day, seeking to focus on the Holy Spirit. Seek, rather, the kingdom of God and His righteousness. Seek Jesus. Seek the Father's will. Seek the path of peace. Seek the next right thing to do. The Holy Spirit will gladly (and imperceptibly) help you with all these things! As you enter into the flow of such a day given over to the pursuit of God, the Holy Spirit becomes at-one with you.

Other people will usually want to be noticed whenever they have gone out of their way to help us, and it is only right to show them generous appreciation. That's good etiquette. The Holy Spirit, however, isn't looking for appreciation. His great desire is to serve the Lord Jesus by effectively serving us. Of course He appreciates it when we notice what He has done and thank Him for it. But the reality is that He is going out of His way to help us *all* of the time. Yet, this is not an onerous task that takes Him away from His preferred desires, it is what He has freely chosen to do. It is what He *loves* doing. That's why He climbed inside of us in the first place!

If we were to thank Him for all that He does, it would leave no room for anything else. That's not His goal. And besides, what would you think of a child who was constantly thanking mother or father for every little thing they did? Might you think the child had too little confidence in the parent's love? Just relax: If you really appreciate Him, He knows.

Who to Pray to?

Do we pray to the Holy Spirit? After all He is fully God. Why not go to Him for everything? The answer may be that we *can*, but it is preferred that we direct our prayers either to the Father or to Jesus. In fact Jesus explicitly states that when it comes to requests, we are to "ask the Father in His Name" or pray directly to our Lord Himself.[3] No reason is given in the text, but a few can be reasonably surmised, the first one being that the Holy Spirit prefers to turn our attention towards the other two, not Himself.[4] Divine etiquette prompts us to abide by the Spirit's desire.

Growing in intimacy with God and Jesus may be additional reasons. Being more or less required to go to the Father for what we need, "forces" us to face the most intimidating Person of the Trinity directly. This grows our relationship with our Father by leading us to discover that He is not as we may have feared Him to be. The fear of God, rightly understood, is immensely helpful to us, but godly fear is too often supplanted in our anxious hearts by a craven fear of God, which fears what He may do, or allow, or ask of us. That kind of fear never comes from God![5] Both Jesus and the Holy Spirit are at work to turn Adam's frightened children around and lead us back to the Father of Light that we tend to keep running away from.[6]

That Jesus invites us to pray to Himself directly surely has to do with cultivating that intimacy of conversation with our Savior and Best Friend which both the Father and the Holy Spirit evidently desire us to enjoy.[7] See if this image helps you get oriented. On those dusty Galilean roads, the disciples spoke with Jesus face to face as they traveled along, bringing Him all their hopes and dreams as well as all their requests. He wants to have that same kind of communion with us as we walk with Him through each day. Then, the Holy Spirit was *with* the disciples, helping them to stay focused on Jesus. Now, that same Spirit is *in* us, helping us to keep our focus on the Lord.[8] In fact, in my limited experience, few things attract the Holy Spirit like praising Jesus in fully focused worship. At those times it seems as if the Holy Spirit comes rushing in like a mighty wind, so great is His desire to honor our Lord.

Grieving, Quenching and Snubbing

Scripture speaks of the Holy Spirit as a dove, perhaps the gentlest of all the winged creatures. Doves by their very nature evoke the peace they have come to symbolize. In a very real sense the Holy Spirit is the peace of Christ which abides with us.[9] Don't we want this gentle dove of peace to rest always upon us as He did with Jesus at His baptism?[10] Then let us take care how we act around Him. Doves are very easy to startle into flight!

We are advised in scripture neither to "grieve" the Holy Spirit nor to "quench" Him.[11] We grieve the Holy Spirit when we take on attitudes against others whom He loves just as much as He loves us. Judging and accusing others, holding resentments against them, and speaking ill of them behind their backs, runs the risk of grieving the Holy Spirit. That's a discernible pain on the inside which can be felt just beyond the hard edge of our anger. It's His way of calling us to return to our first love and the commitment to mercy which got us started.

Quenching the Spirit is what can happen when we resist what He desires to do through us. Naturally, we probably all miss a lot of what He desires to do (or our lives would look radically more like that of Jesus), but quenching happens over things He has repeatedly demonstrated to us. To ignore a prompting He has trained us to notice, often results in a sudden feeling of deflation, as if the wind had gone out of our sails. This may have been because we were already tired and just couldn't "be bothered," or we pulled back due to the challenge level of what He is asking, or we stubbornly insisted upon our own way.

Snubbing the Spirit is admittedly a non-Biblical term which is being used here to denote a most serious breach of etiquette when thinking about the Holy Spirit. It is acting as if He is somehow less of a person than we are. I'm not sure what effect this has upon Him, but I am quite sure it does us a great deal of mischief to think of our mysterious Guest as being less than human. The problem here is that our cultural conditioning has been training us to think of spirit as an impersonal "force" or benevolent power, something nebulous and ill-defined.

When people talk of "spirituality," this seems to be what they have in mind. Yet, when Jesus said that God is *Spirit*, He could not have meant the limitations which we ordinarily place upon that term, for Jesus is Himself God and therefore fully Spirit. Our God has emotion, intellect and will, not in any fallen way, but heightened by perfection and filled with glory. He who made us in His Image and gives life to each one of us, cannot be less than we are. Whatever it is that we mean by soul, personhood and personality, God is that and more. In *Mere Christianity* C. S. Lewis addressed this gap in our perceptions.

> *A good many people nowadays say, "I believe in a God, but not in a personal God." They feel that the mysterious something which is behind all other things must be more than a person. Now the Christians quite agree. But the Christians are the only people who offer any idea of what a being that is beyond personality could be like. All the other people, though they say that God is beyond personality, really think of Him as something impersonal: that is, as something less than personal.*[12]

If we are to think rightly of the Holy Spirit we must imagine Him as a Person, one of the Three Persons of the Godhead. It would be bad form indeed to think of Him as a mere power or force: *Never* refer to the Third Person as an "It"! Nor, would it be Biblically correct to use any other personal pronoun than the male when referring to Him. The Holy Spirit is described both as the Spirit of the Father and the Spirit sent from Jesus.[13] Just as we are clearly intended to think of the Father as male and just as surely as Jesus is now forever the God-*man*, so the scriptures leave no option but to think of the Holy Spirit in male, not female, terms. Why this might be so, can be debated or explored, but we must at least acknowledge that we are not the creators of our revelation, but merely the receivers of it. It's good etiquette to address people according to their stated preference, especially divine Persons.

Solitude, Silence and Serenity

If you wish to keep the divine dove resting upon you, learn to avoid grieving, quenching and snubbing the Spirit, but above all, seek to cultivate a resting place within your own heart. Make friends with solitude, silence and serenity. A more inviting landing zone for the Holy Spirit can hardly be imagined. This may require working with the Lord to gain a few divine reversals in how you perceive these three states, now that Christ has come into your life.

In solitude, we are no longer alone for He is always with us, therefore we need never give way to loneliness. In silence, the eternal Word is always speaking good things to our soul, therefore we need never rely upon others to build us up. In serenity, the real work of the world remains in His Hands while we do the one work required of us, therefore we need never succumb to anxiety and business.[14] Admittedly, these are not easy lessons to learn, but it gives the Holy Spirit great pleasure if we sign up for His course of instruction.

Being content to live with Him in the peace of interior solitude, silence and serenity is the best etiquette of all. May the river of peace that flows in us through Him carry you into great adventures of life and ministry!

Holy Spirit

SPIRIT LED MINISTRY

For it is God who works in you,
both to will and to work for his good pleasure.
Philippians 2:13

CHAPTER 13

MINISTRY TO OTHERS

There are two great adventures to this new life in Christ: getting to know our God better and joining Him in the Rescue. We all get to play a part! Of course only Jesus can save people, as we have found out by our own experience. But He delights in gifting us, training us and going out with us to seek and save those who are lost or hurting in any way.

> **His intention was the perfecting and the full equipping of the saints (His consecrated people), [that they should do] the work of ministering toward building up Christ's body (the church).**
> Ephesians 4:12 AMP

Ministry to others is such great good fun (most of the time) that it can almost become addictive. There are so many outstanding things about it: cultivating the heart of a servant, participating in the camaraderie of good fellowship, discovering and developing your gifts for ministry, learning the art of divine guidance, working side by side with the Holy Spirit, and being uplifted by a wholesome sense of purpose. Best of all are those moments of spontaneous worship, when the work really hits the spot of blessing in someone's life and you both go flying up into praise. What's not to like about it? Well, it's not all peaches and cream, but for now let's take it in faith that you're going to love it so much that a caution is needed right at the starting gate.

Before You Even Start

Ministering to others is immensely rewarding and greatly needed, but it is our secondary calling.[1] Unless this is clearly understood, the attempt to be of service will eventually lead to chaos, burn out, or hard feelings. Our primary purpose and our number one assignment is learning how to love the Lord with our whole heart in all our moments and in all our situations. The Lord packed a lot into the "first and greatest" command, but among other things it means that if we put loving and seeking Him first, the other things will fall into place. [2]

> **And he said to him, "You shall love the Lord your God with all your heart and with all your soul and with all your mind. 38 This is the great and first commandment. 39 And a second is like it: You shall love your neighbor as yourself."** Matthew 22:37-39

In practical terms the order of the two great commandments indicates that we have to stay under Jesus' leadership (the first command) while we are trying to be of service to others (the second command). In seeking to be under His leadership, our primary concern is to make sure that we are trusting Jesus with what He allows and following Him in what He asks.[3] If this sounds difficult, then that should show just how much this on-the-job training is necessary.

There is almost a universal tendency to see the needs of the people we are serving as our primary concern, but the Lord always sees the condition of our heart as His primary concern for us:[4] Are we trusting Him (or stressing); are we enjoying the peace of His fellowship as we work; and are we letting the Spirit of love lead us? Few workplace bosses would care about the internal state of their workers, only the external results. Our Lord is radically different.

This difference has a lovely dimension to it for it means that results are not what we are being graded on as we seek to serve others. Love is. Our love for Him, and through Him, our love for others: Is it growing? Saint Teresa of Avila wrote that "God doesn't care nearly so much about the work we do as the love with which we do it."[5] What this means is that the wide field of ministry to others is secretly God's great laboratory for cultivating in us listening ears, trusting hearts, willing spirits and loving ways. Knowing this up front gives us enhanced opportunities for cooperating with the lessons.

Now, Where to Begin?

This is the easy part. Pray, then jump right in. Almost always you will find open doors for service and people in leadership who are willing to give you a try, if you are willing to take the lowest place.[6] Starting at the bottom makes great sense. It gives you time to learn the ropes—how things are done in that particular field of ministry. It also leaves you free of heavier responsibilities to learn how to pray as you work. Christian work always needs lots of prayer: for practical help, for heart attitudes, for inspired ideas, for breakthroughs, and for the leadership. Be particularly watchful in prayer over your own heart attitudes. Remember the two "golden rules" of service:

1) Kindness: You can't always help someone the way they want you to, but you can always BE KIND to them. Being kind helps everyone. Few things speak the love of God better than when we show patience and kindness to someone whose attitude doesn't deserve anything but reproach.

2) Respect: You will not always agree with the leadership, but you can always GIVE RESPECT to them. David was respectful of the wicked king Saul who was trying to kill him. Christian leaders won't try to kill you, but they definitely aren't all saints either. Make sure you don't stone them for their clay feet.

The great advantage in getting started with anything available is that the Lord can steer you better, if you have some forward movement going. Having a sense of peace about what you are doing is all that really matters in the beginning. As you go along God will begin to give you clues that will point you towards your future calling and assignment.

Notice what emerges in your heart. Are there aspects to the work that particularly energize or inspire you? Are there certain kinds of people or situations of need that tug on your heart more? The former give you insight into your ministry gift and the latter gives you vision for your field of ministry. In the beginning, while I was still folding tables and putting chairs away for others, I found myself thinking about what I would say if I had the opportunity to teach. I also noticed how much I wanted to help others with their emotional needs. Eventually, I entered into the reality I had been dreaming about.

Meditate on what people say to you, especially if it was unsolicited by you. Those you serve will often thank you in a way that emphasizes the kind of ministry they received from the Lord through you. That's a powerful indication of your ministry gift.[7] Also, leaders may comment on the gifts that they see operating in you, especially when they are talking over what you might want to do next around the church.

As time goes on your sense of calling will deepen, or you will find questions stirring in you about what your purpose is and how to prepare for it. No one can fully teach you these things except the Lord, but fortunately He is with you. And He has had plenty of experience at training new recruits, so carry all of your questions to Him and watch as the answers begin to unfold. In the meantime, let the following chapters help you gain a general understanding of the key issues of calling and purpose, gifting and training. But first a final word of caution.

The Big Hurdle to Clear

Be on guard against offense. Never let it build up. Always go to work on your heart when offense comes and make no mistake about it, offense will come. What's more, it will most likely come in a way you least expect, causing you to feel entirely justified in holding on to it. You would still be wrong. You have an enemy who doesn't want you being of service to the Lord, but he especially doesn't want you to become a *loving* servant. We may have the best of hearts and the best of intentions, but watch out! The only way you and I can become truly loving is by learning how to forgive all manner of injury, mistreatment and wrong—just as Jesus does. That's why every would-be servant of Jesus has to be tried in the fire of offense.

What do you do? Forgive! Forgive until you are holding nothing but a desire for the other person's well-being. Forgive until you get your heart back for them.[8] This will be relatively easy most of the time, but tough as nails sometimes, or you are not (yet) being seriously tested. Call vigorously on the Lord so that you can learn from Him how to release hurt or hard feelings and accept people as they are.[9] Let Jesus be your model and your inspiration for how to respond to offense.[10] This is the growth upwards into Christ that the

Father desires to cultivate in you.[11] We can be sure He practiced what He preached.

And whenever you stand praying, forgive, if you have anything against anyone, so that your Father also who is in heaven may forgive you your trespasses." Mark 11:25

As you learn to keep your heart free and clear of offense, you will discover that the Lord will always have something worthwhile for you to do. He only puts us on the shelf if our hearts get hard. That's not going to happen to you, now that you are on guard against it. So pray, look for an open door, and jump right in. The water's fine!

Holy Spirit

CHAPTER 14

PREPARING FOR MINISTRY

Considering the Lord's high standards, you might think it takes a long time to get ready to do ministry. For some things, yes, a fair amount of training may be required, but for most things all you need is a heart and the willingness to jump into that sea of human need, lostness and misery which surrounds you. Nevertheless, you will be tested on the job concerning these basics, so be sure you know what they are and have them in play.

For you were called to freedom, brothers. Only do not use your freedom as an opportunity for the flesh, but through love serve one another. Galatians 5:13

Ministry Basics: Love

Mastering the basics is crucial for success in any field of endeavor. Whether you want to be a ball player, a musician, or a farmer the most important thing is how well you do it and for that you have to be good at the basics. That's not the way it is with Christian ministry. Naturally, it matters that you learn to do your tasks well, but that is far from being the most important thing. Relationships are the main thing! That's because our number one task is love. Relationships are, therefore, "the basics" we have to master.

And if I have prophetic powers, and understand all mysteries and all knowledge, and if I have all faith, so as to remove mountains, but have not love, I am nothing. If I give away all I have, and if I deliver up my body to be burned, but have not love, I gain nothing. 1 Corinthians 13:2-3

Here are some examples taken from real life: If you fed a hundred hungry people, but treated one of them rudely, you set the work back in everyone's eyes. If you serve the people well enough, but harbor ill will towards a fellow minister you are a stumbling block to the rest of the team. If you are treating everyone with respect and efficiency, but are drifting from the peace of Christ into burnout, you have lost your first Love.

The Lord sets a top priority on love. He wants us to put loving others ahead of any work we are doing for them in His Name.[1] He takes the lead in this for the whole time that we are serving others, He is at work loving and serving us. In fact He is so good at rewarding us that His peace and joy flow in our midst like living water.[2] Nevertheless, if we don't do things His way, those same waters can quickly run dry. Go at Christian ministry pushing your own agenda or trusting in your own abilities and you can easily over-fill with stress. That's not His way. Imagine Jesus feeding the five thousand or healing the multitudes. Does He look worried or anxious? Not at all. The ones who lost their peace are the disciples, a name which means learners. That's us!

Learning how to live in His peace and joy while we serve Him is actually a major key to loving the ones we serve. Think over the many times you have been on the receiving end of someone else's service. If they were impatient, how did that make you feel? If they were in a sour mood, were you happy you walked into their shop? It is so easy to forget this when we are the ones trying to move mountains of difficulty for the sake of the Rescue, but the simple truth is only love *ministers* to others.

Three Primary Relationships

Christian ministry is, therefore, one of the best ways in which to grow a truly loving heart. There are three main relationships that the Lord wants to help us build as we seek to be of service. If we work on these relationships the right way (His way), we will grow in love and He will be able to build the work around us and do His best work through us. These three relationships are the people we serve, our fellow servants and the Lord Himself. The kind of love that is grown and the practical test of that love is different in each area.

I. The People We Serve

Love to cultivate: love as compassion.
The test of love: Are you being kind?

God's love is not primarily a squishy emotion that we feel in our hearts. Thank goodness He does give us feelings of immense affection for others *at times*. When we experience them it is always energizing and delightful, but they do not last. You simply cannot build a lifetime of ministry to people based on feelings that come and go. What we always have with us, however, is the Example of Jesus (who is love in action) and the definition of love He gives us in His Word. Please notice that not one of the following characteristics is a feeling. By God's own definition, you and I do not have to emote at all. He isn't asking us to feel love, but to *do* it!

Love is patient and kind; love does not envy or boast; it is not arrogant or rude. It does not insist on its own way; it is not irritable or resentful; it does not rejoice at wrongdoing, but rejoices with the truth. Love bears all things, believes all things, hopes all things, endures all things. 1 Corinthians 13:4-7

Because love is not primarily a feeling, God can (and does) command us to love.[3] We are to love "our neighbors" and that certainly includes the people we are seeking to serve. Nevertheless, you can breathe a sigh of relief that He does not expect you to feel love when you don't. At those times the best approach is to do what love would want you to do. Heidi Baker, a missionary in Mozambique, asks, "What would love look like in action?" God's love is practical. It is eminently doable.

Now let's turn this definition around. The people we serve won't care what we feel for them (in our better moments), if we are treating them with disrespect or impatience (in their moment). Kindness is our prime directive. You may not feel any love or have what they need, but if you are kind to them *they* will feel the love and be grateful. It remains true, however, that feelings of love bring an inner release of energy, power and delight. It is also true that God has placed His own love inside of us. Wouldn't it be great if we could learn how to tap into the vast reservoir of love and flow in its power? Indeed we can! There are two tried and proven ways of "releasing the Spirit" for loving service.

1) Take out the garbage. Just as clear water will not flow through sludge-filled pipes, so the Holy Spirit requires us to keep our hearts cleansed of judgment and anger, fear and worry, doubt and depression. Otherwise, grace recedes and the joy killers take over. When that happens, negative emotions block love at the starting gate. Forgive, let go, and cast all accumulated cares on Jesus. As you empty out of what doesn't belong in you, the Holy Spirit will fill and lift you once again.

2) Focus on compassion. This is one of the great lessons we receive by watching Jesus doing ministry in the scriptures. Many times what moved His Heart to deeds of love was the compassion which welled up within Him at the sight of human distress. So it is with us. What moved the heart of Jesus will also move our own. Whenever you need to recover fresh strength, look deep into the ocean of suffering in front of you. Get your spiritual eyes off of everything else and refocus on what moved you in the first place: compassion.[4]

II. Our Fellow Servants

Love to cultivate: love as acceptance.
The test of love: Are you forgiving?

In doing ministry we often have to work side by side with other believers. This is by the Lord's design and it gives us wonderful moments of close fellowship. It also gives us unavoidable opportunities for being rubbed the wrong way! That is also by the Lord's doing. Jesus never causes offense to occur, or desires it to come, but He definitely will make good use of it when it shows up.

The first thing to notice about being offended with fellow workers is that it is harder to forgive them than the people we serve. In the latter's case we are well aware of their need and their struggles. That's why we volunteered to serve them. We don't expect good Christian behavior from them, either because they are lost to begin with, or because their suffering takes precedence. Our feelings of compassion for them are, therefore, much stronger, more readily moving us to forgive them and find excuses for their behavior.

None of this applies to our fellow servants, at least not in the same measure. We naturally hold them to a higher standard—the one we ourselves are trying to live by. Since they are professing to be Christians, we expect them to act like it. We don't want to excuse or forgive them. We want them corrected! We didn't get on the team with them because we felt compassion for them, so we have little compassion to give. To make matters worse, because we are working closely with them, we see their flaws repeatedly. We may even be wounded by their words or wrong ways: "Friction burns" sensitize us against further injury. All of this can make it harder to forgive and accept them as they are.

Now take these problems with fellow workers and compound them, if the ones who offend us are our leaders. They should know better and set a better example. Their weaknesses really do hinder the work. Yet, leaders are notoriously hard to correct from below and seem resistant to both words and prayers. You can sometimes speak with fellow workers and they will adjust their behavior; less frequently the leaders. To top it off, we tend to elevate leaders to pedestals of perfection no one could possibly occupy, and then are doubly dismayed when they fall from the heights. Take heart! All of this is part of the Lord's plan for training you in His ways.[5]

For our love to be *His* love it has to pass through the fires of offense. We simply must learn how to forgive as He does, which is everyone at all times, including flawed fellow workers and failed Christian leaders.[6] He has forgiven you for all that is wrong with you, past and present, hasn't He? He accepts you just as you are, doesn't He? He is willing to use you in ministry, despite your many weaknesses and failings, isn't He? Well, He is dead serious about you giving the same grace to others![7]

It is for our own good. Not only do we want to become great lovers of humanity like our merciful Lord, we also yearn to live in the "joy unspeakable" He makes available.[8] You can't have joy and hold onto unforgiveness at the same time. To be a happy Pharisee is constitutionally impossible! So when offense comes (and it will), drag your heart to the cross (as He did) and do all the forgiving, releasing and accepting there that love requires. You will grow by leaps and bounds.

III. The Lord, Our Master

Love to cultivate: love as obedience.
The test of love: Are you trusting?

We serve a Leader we can't see. This has unique problems all its own. The One we are meant to follow in life and in ministry is invisible to us. We "see" Him by faith, but few of us see Him with our own two eyes. If we were walking with Peter and John on those Galilean roads, we would see Jesus turning to the left and immediately realize we have a decision to make: Will I follow Him there? If He sent us to the next village with instructions, everyone including ourselves would know if we obeyed His words: Did you buy the bread? It is not nearly so clear for us in this time and place.

With earthly leaders we can at least look at their expression and know if we are pleasing them or exasperating them. If we can't tell by their looks, they'll let us know. Good leaders give you feedback. They want to cultivate you as a follower. They want to develop your gifts for service. They want to make good use of your time. They try to give you clear directions. Jesus is the best Leader on the planet, but we can neither see Him visibly nor hear Him audibly (most of the time). How does He make up for this?

The short answer is that if you and I really want to know His will in any situation, He has ways of helping us find out.[9] The long answer is that it takes time and trouble to learn how to trust, listen to, and follow a leader who keeps playing Hide and Seek with you! Ok, so why does He do it this way? To grow love in us. Whoa. That's an unexpected answer, but it has to be the right one, since His primary command to us is that we learn to love Him at all times and in all situations. That certainly includes ministry. In fact ministry is a great way to grow a genuine love for Him, because seeking to be His servant requires us to seek His will.

At every point of decision we have a choice: Will I seek His will to do things His way, or will I handle it my way? Love (in God) gives us that choice. Love (in us) takes that choice, turns from Self and seeks to obey Jesus. Our primary relationship in ministry is as a servant to a Master. This is the entry level—He will want to raise us into friendship eventually, but we must first learn to be disciples (followers).[10] We draw close as servants by seeking to follow our Leader in all things. We not only want to do His will, we want to do it His way. This enables Him to work in us and through us whenever we are on track. If we want results, we have to seek Him. If we want to love Him, we must learn to obey Him. He calls obedience love.[11] We have three main ways in which our obedience to Him is enabled and tested.

1) His Word. Do you trust Him enough to obey His Word and live within its boundaries? His Word gives positive general directions and clearly marks out the moral boundaries we are to live within. Serving Him means bringing all of our ways into obedience to His Word.

2) His Spirit. Do you trust Him enough to allow His Spirit to lift, lead and guide you? The Lord will give you a sense of the next right thing to be done. That may not fit into your plans, but it does His. The Holy Spirit guides us by His peace. If we take the step He is pointing to there is peace; if we keep love and trust in our hearts there is peace. That's our "go" signal![12]

3) Earthly authorities. Do you trust Him enough to obey the ones He has placed over you?[13] We are not to blindly follow people who are asking something immoral or illegal of us, but most Christian leaders operate within the wide boundaries of the law. Their way of going at things may not be your way, it may not even be God's best way, but we are still meant to give them the best measure of service that we can.

These three great loves—for the people we serve, the people we serve with, and for Jesus Himself—don't grow all by themselves. Or rather, they do grow by an effortless grace when conditions are right, but if we don't cultivate them in adverse circumstances, our harvest will be mostly weeds and rotten fruit! God starts us with a lot of grace, but we have to learn how to work with His love and mercy in order for things to keep growing in the right direction. So, be prepared to refresh your compassion, acceptance and obedience when the manure of unwanted events and difficult people gets added into the mix.

CHAPTER 15

CALLING AND PURPOSE

Because God calls us into relationships of love, we have not one, but two magnificent purposes to discover: 1) the joy of knowing Him intimately and 2) the unique way He designed us to be of loving service to others. These pursuits supply endless fascination! If our life is not characterized by discovery and adventure, we are probably missing the mark on both counts. As we enter more deeply into our purpose, convergence carries us ever closer to destiny.

I press on toward the goal for the prize of the upward call of God in Christ Jesus. Philippians 3:14

Double Duties, Double Delights

There need never be a dull moment walking with Jesus. He has given us two engrossing and fascinating assignments: He calls us to His side to a) know and love Him and b) love and serve others. These two great commands actually describe our calling, our purpose, our assignments and our destiny. We may think of them as duties, but they are also intended to be our delights. Nothing could be more heart-expanding and joy-inducing than to pursue these two great callings.

And he said to him, "You shall love the Lord your God with all your heart and with all your soul and with all your mind. This is the great and first commandment. And a second is like it: You shall love your neighbor as yourself. On these two commandments depend all the Law and the Prophets." Matthew 22:37-40

These are certainly commands, but they are also promises. If you look far enough into the future you will see by eyes of faith that one Day this will be eternally true for all of us who make it home to heaven. We will become the people who know what it is like to fully and fantastically love God with our whole heart and who love the entire Body of Christ that He is calling into His eternal family. That's our destiny! God has decreed that He will accomplish it for us: We "shall" enter into the perfection of love which heaven fulfills.[1] How much of it will we enter into in this life? That depends upon our willingness to go for broke, betting the farm on Jesus and living for Him, rather than for ourselves alone.[2]

Unquestionably, loving God is our number one assignment—it is the "great and first" command. Since this section is on ministry, our focus here is on the second commandment, loving our neighbor as ourselves. Right away we can see from the Lord's description that one key to actually loving others depends upon how we love ourselves. Many of us don't love for ourselves! Truth be told, we are angry, frustrated, demanding and impatient with ourselves. This cannot help but spill over into the way we treat other people.[3] Once we learn to love ourselves the right way, we no longer need others to meet our emotional needs. This sets us free to love and serve them with no strings attached, just as God does us.

Now we can focus on what it means to love our neighbor. Having a heart full of love for others is a good thing. However, that really won't do our neighbor any practical good. All it takes is one look into the sea of lost, hurting humanity around us to realize that other people need help and lots of it. If we have any love at all, we will want to be part of the Rescue.[4] Some need to be saved by coming to know the Lord; others need physical, emotional and material assistance. Every individual and every people group needs help of some kind.

Called with a Purpose

There's no end to human need! This makes it easy to begin, but how do we find where we can best be of service? We probably all have a sense that God has us here for a reason, a special purpose. Usually this is completely misunderstood. Nothing could be more important to the Lord than that we enter into our high calling of knowing Him—that's our greatest delight and highest purpose.[5] Just the same this isn't what people usually mean when they say "I know God has me here for a reason."[6] They're thinking of some way of being of service to humanity. That's why our first step into our calling and purpose needs to be discovering what our Number One reason for being here is and understanding how to pursue it. Jesus has already warned us that until we get that one in place everything else will be out of order.[7] With that sizable piece in place we are ready to look at the rest of the puzzle.

Our calling by God includes a form-fitted way of serving Him in the lives of other people. Some people have a sense of what that is from an early age. They just know they want to be doctors, farmers or musicians, etc. and never waver from that goal all their lives. Even unbelievers who don't know the Lord or want to know Him, may have this sense of direction which comes from God. They just won't say it's a calling, because that implies that there is a God who has a claim on them and they don't want to answer His call. But what of us who know that our God is gloriously Alive, can speak for Himself, and has a great plan for our life? Sometimes we can wander in the wilderness for years, never discovering our special purpose. *That seems so unfair!*

Fortunately, there are ways of finding out what our special purpose is. These are tried and proven ways, but none of them are guaranteed to work on their own apart from God. The Lord is sovereign. He has His own ways of dealing with us and He knows only too well how quick we are to wriggle off the hook. What hooks us in terms of service is wanting to know our special calling and gifts. Of course He wants us to know those things too, but He also may be interested in helping us learn how to be guided by Him while He has our attention. Additionally, He may want to check out the true level of our surrender to Him, as in "God I will do anything for you, but…"[8] If you want to walk with the Lord you have to get off your "buts"!

1) Nudges. What tugs at your heart? In your head you may have all kinds of ideas about how humanity needs to be helped.[9] The Lord is far more interested in growing love, so look to your heart. What situations of human need actually move you to tears, or to deep feelings of compassion? Jesus Himself was often moved to specific ministry on the basis of compassion for the human suffering He saw. Therefore, we can expect that God will draw us into our fields of harvest the same way. Learning the way of the heart does not come easily to many Westerners. That's why seeking our calling gives the Lord such excellent teaching opportunities.

2) Drawings. What people group(s) are you drawn to? Paul had a dream in which a man called him to come to Macedonia.[10] God still calls us to people groups, though the ways we hear it are varied. People groups come in all sizes and shapes. Those with an evangelist's calling will constantly be thinking about people who need to be saved. They may narrow it down even more with their concern for unsaved people of a certain region, ethnic group, or age group. Other people will find themselves thinking about how kids in the inner city could be helped, if someone would work with them during after school hours. Or, you may just love talking with the "old folks" and only need to see some practical way to link up your heart attachment with something that looks like service.

3) Gifts. What gifts are you discovering? As we try our hand at various ways of serving people we inevitably discover what we are good at (and not so good at). Let your strengths lead you.[11] Things that come easily to you are a sign of prior giftedness from the Lord. So is affirmation from the people you work with as well as from the ones you serve. Other people will notice and affirm gifts operating in you that you might be totally unaware of. These in turn will point you towards your ultimate main channels of service. This is why it matters less where we start serving, than that we start. Once we get going the Lord can more readily steer us.

4) Listening. Are you learning the way of guidance? We have not just been given a Book to follow, as helpful as that is. Our guide in life is none other than the Lord Himself. Jesus still calls us to follow Him, just as surely and as intimately as the original invitation came to those first disciples in Galilee. Jesus may have dropped out of sight—we don't get to see His steps as they did—but in exchange He has given His Spirit to live within us. Entering into the fullness of our calling, inescapably means entering into the fullness of new life in the Holy Spirit. Learning to be guided by the Holy Spirit is, therefore, essential for the pursuit of our calling.

Convergence

Making all of this come together is the Lord's work. Our part is to be surrendered and committed to Him, courageous at following His guidance, and to listen in a searching way to our own heart.[12] Deep is calling to deep.[13] If we keep answering the call, He will lead and draw us through many unforeseeable events which will both grow and guide us. Eventually, God willing, we will emerge from all the training into a season in life where our gift set comes together with our sense of calling. Our destined purpose draws near!

In this season—it's called convergence—work actually becomes play. We end up doing what we have been designed by God to do best and may even get paid for it. Amazing. But be forewarned: One study found that only a very small percentage of pastors could say that they were experiencing convergence. Most felt that they had not entered into the best use of their gifts or had somehow become sidelined along the way. These are the people we expect to have the surest sense of calling![14]

Don't let anything discourage you. You are not them. It all hangs on just how far you want to go in following Jesus. Be determined to go the distance, to the last measure of sacrifice and surrender, and He will lead you into the promised land of convergence and destiny.

Holy Spirit

CHAPTER 16

THE SCHOOL OF THE SPIRIT

There are lessons of the Lord which can be described in a classroom, but can only be imparted by the Spirit in the school of daily life. Being trained for ministry includes character development and spiritual growth, so expect on the job training to continue no matter what you are doing. That means leaning to survive trials and eventually thrive in the midst of them. Fortunately for all of us, our Teacher is also our Comforter and Best Friend.

"I am the true vine, and my Father is the vinedresser. Every branch of mine that does not bear fruit he takes away, and every branch that does bear fruit he prunes, that it may bear more fruit." John 15:1-2

Internal Instruction

Without a doubt the Holy Spirit is the best Teacher on earth.[1] Nothing escapes His attention. He is always working to help us do our best and be our best. If you have ever watched the Olympics, then you have probably seen athletes huddle up with their coaches after events. Even if they did spectacularly well, the coach will whisper words to them about how to improve for the next set. Similarly, the Holy Spirit will frequently bring to your mind ways in which you can improve your game as a servant of others. He has a lot to teach us!

Fortunately, the Lord is pleased with any step we take in the right direction and He never reproaches us for missteps, but He loves us too much to let us get the big head. Helping others leaves us open to temptation by pride because, after all, our good works are on public display. Naturally we want to do well—and He desires that for us too—but there is a hidden danger in success: taking credit to ourselves, or thinking that we have arrived at a pinnacle of achievement. So, expect it that your greatest encourager is also your most devoted critic.[2]

Not only is the Lord keenly interested in cultivating our abilities, He also wants to preserve our humility, so that we will remain teachable. If we are open to it, we are now learners for life in the great, never-ending School of the Spirit. This can keep everything that we do fresh and exciting for we who enroll in this course of instruction are always seeking to grow better at loving people and more effective at serving them. It can also open doors (if you let it) for the enemy to harass or oppress you with self-condemning thoughts.[3] Learning to separate out conviction by the Spirit from condemnation by the enemy is part of the on the job training we need.

Nine Lessons

This list is not all-inclusive. It's simply an overview of certain basic lessons that the Lord will likely be working on with you as you work with Him.

1) Connection. Just as batteries don't last long without a re-charge, none of us can stay "in the Spirit" and advance the kingdom without staying closely connected to the One who desires to work through us.[4] Jesus has given us five main ways of connecting to Him. Service is one of those ways, but staying refreshed and ready for anything means that we will need to learn how to keep the other four in good working condition: Bible, prayer, worship and fellowship. You will learn, if you are open to the lessons, that no matter how much you have to do for the Lord, the most important thing is staying well-connected to Him. It's our #1 assignment.

2) Criticism. Just because we are stepping out of our complacency or our comfort zones to do something noble for the Lord, doesn't mean critics, naysayers and busybodies will leave us alone. If they bother you, don't waste time trying to change them (or worse, becoming a complainer yourself). You could sooner bail out the ocean than change the sea of humanity around you. Let the barrage of negativity from others (when it happens) turn you away from seeking to please people and re-focus on

Jesus and how He sees you. Are you here to please others or God? Criticism can help you see things about yourself you need to work on, even if the only thing that needs changing is your reaction to it.

3) Dependence. Entering into the Lord's work usually means discovering how little we have to bring to the table, like the disciples must have felt when asked by Jesus to feed the multitude. Seen from the outside we almost never seem to have enough: More money is needed for the work, or more resources, or more people. Seen from the inside, we can't help but notice our weaknesses and inadequacies. This is likely an uncomfortable position for many of us in the beginning, but it is teaching the life-long lesson of depending upon the Lord to be our faithful Source and supply.

4) Guidance. We may be perfectly willing to say with Jesus, "Behold, I come to do Your will" and yet not have a clue how to place ourselves under His leadership.[5] If we are willing to begin at the lowest level, serving the Lord's will is easy: Just place yourself under the leaders He has already placed over the work. Eventually, though, you will start seeing needs that you would like to reach out to directly. This naturally causes us to pray and seek the Lord for guidance. Learn to watch for the opportunities His Hands provide and listen for the ideas He brings you. Guidance is an art best learned on the job, not in the arm chair.

5) Waiting. No one likes waiting these days. There is so much hurry up and impatience all around. Yet, waiting on God is a huge theme in the Bible, especially in the Old Testament.[6] Waiting is akin to hope and is infused with faith that the things we had to commit to the Lord (because they aren't happening now!) will come in due time, if we persevere while we are waiting. Christian ministry teaches us to be patient a) because without patience we will inevitably become unkind and that will never do, and b) so many things have to be prayed for in order for the Lord to bring them about. There's no point in holding your breath or drumming your fingers when what needs doing requires the Spirit's wooing in someone else's life. God's timing cannot be forced, especially since His priority is working on hearts. As you learn to wait, be sure to learn how to "enter into His rest" and "possess your soul" with patience.[7]

6) Weakness.[8] Don't we love leading with our strengths? Don't we wish we didn't have any weaknesses getting in the way? Strengths are a joy. We can get things done with them! Weaknesses are a bother all the way around. Nevertheless, the call of the Lord brings us face to face with our weakness, time and time again. Why? Wouldn't we be better off without them? In fact we would do well to learn to see weaknesses as friends in disguise, not enemies to be feared. Our weaknesses lead us to Christ, reminding us to pray, to cast our hope on Him, and to cling to Him. Strengths usually throw us back into total reliance upon ourselves. Weaknesses teach us the high and holy way of dependence upon the Lord.

7) Busyness. Jesus said He needed to be about His Father's "business."[9] He never said He needed to be busy. Busyness is a modern plague. For those who have caught the bad infection it feels good—most of the time. It really feels like one is making progress at getting things done. But what happened to the peace of Christ? What happened to the leadership of the Holy Spirit? What about the people who were steam-rolled as you pressed your agenda forward? The one who has learned the ways of the Lord gets more done with less effort, because the Holy Spirit is supplying strength and synchronizing events. Busyness is like an overfilled cup of coffee, sure to scorch someone when it's spilled, most frequently the holder. Let the Lord teach you when enough is enough.[10]

8) Rescuing. There is only room for One Rescuer on the team.[11] That position is already filled! Jesus cares for each individual we are trying to serve infinitely more than we ever will, but He has His own way of working with them and His own timing about it. We can easily get in His way if we seize things to ourselves, trying to fix people in our own strength.[12] Learn to let your hand rest lightly on your plans and your desires.[13] God often rules by over-ruling us. This is frustrating, but necessary. He knows what He's doing; we don't. At the same time the enemy loves to obstruct and oppose the work. When do we submit to God; when do we resist the devil? This calls for real discernment. Patient perseverance usually wins the day, though the victory may come days later than you originally expected.

9) Submission. We are to "submit to one another" keeping the "unity of the Spirit in the bond of peace."[14] Here is where the rubber of gospel truth meets the hard road of daily life. There are so many bumps in the road when it comes to working with others! Yet, the most important thing about the work is the relationships: with the people being served, with fellow workers and with our leaders in the field. The Holy Spirit is watching carefully over all of this. Of course He hates it when we are mistreated, abused or oppressed, but neither is there any place in Christian ministry for us to adopt an attitude of self-pity, wounded pride, or resentment. Learn to be far less concerned about how you are treated, than how you treat others.[15]

Tests and Trials

There is a difference between tests and trials. Without drawing too fine a distinction, let's just say that tests represent the kinds of situations we face most days. Seeking to be of service will test us in the various ways listed above, among others. Be ready for pop quizzes. Life hands them out all the time! Staying connected to the Lord and talking things over with experienced friends takes care of most things. You will find yourself learning all kinds of lessons through the ordinary cycle of trouble and resolution. These are usually felt as minor disturbances in the flow of work and as fairly normal emotional reactions. Above it all we usually have a sense of passing the tests and growing in faith and grace.

Trials, however, are more difficult and disturbing. We usually have a feeling of being caught in them, of regressing to previous levels of weakness, and of being too piercingly aware of our moral shortcomings. We don't feel like we are passing at all. In fact it is the

Lord who passes the test of any trial worthy of being called a trial.[16] He proves His strength of heart to us: His faithfulness and His mercy triumph over our dilemma and lead us out. This takes time. If (or when) you get caught in a trial, try to remember that He only disciplines in love. Once you recover your trust and confidence in God—at a new level—the trial has done its work.

Neither tests, nor trials, are a sign of His displeasure. He is genuinely pleased that you are seeking to serve Him. He loves you and He is really, really easy to please. Trials and tests are His strange way of working with us to liberate us in areas of our life where words alone could never have accomplished the work.[17] He takes us through experiences that we might have shunned before we decided to follow Him, or overlooked by primarily being focused on ourselves, rather than the needs of others. He is delighted to have us on his team. He wishes to reward us for our service with greater freedom and with a closer walk with Him. Therefore, He disciplines or trains us through tests and trials. It is actually a profound sign of His favor, though a hard one (at times) to interpret.

My child, don't reject the Lord's discipline, and don't be upset when he corrects you. For the Lord corrects those he loves, just as a father corrects a child in whom he delights. Proverbs 3:11-12 NLT

CHAPTER 17

TALENT, FRUIT AND GIFTS

The Lord gives talents and natural abilities to everyone as a way of getting us started in life. You don't have to be a believer to be a receiver of these—just develop what you notice. As believers, though, it helps to know the limits of these natural abilities in the spiritual life. Wiser still would be to shift our attention towards cultivating those gifts and fruit which are unique to who we now are in Christ as His new creations.

Therefore, if anyone is in Christ, he is a new creation. The old has passed away; behold, the new has come. 2 Corinthians 5:17

A Progression

In general talents are natural abilities given to everyone at birth, fruit are the good things anyone can cultivate, but gifts are the supernatural way God uniquely works in those who are united to Him through faith in Christ. There may be no hard and fast rules here, but there is a general progression that can be noted. Typically, for those who receive genuine faith in Christ at a very early age, these distinctions will be clouded, since natural abilities, fruit and gifts will begin to appear simultaneously. With adult conversion we see a progression more clearly: Natural abilities and most fruit can appear before conversion; some fruit and most gifts can only appear after conversion.

I. Natural Abilities

We now know that we receive a genetic package at conception which contains fabulous gifts of accumulated generational inheritance. Within it are all of our potential talents waiting (so to speak) for us to discover and cultivate. No one needs to be a believer in God to receive these gifts. Through conception God gives lavishly to everyone natural abilities of body, mind, heart and personality.[1]

We all have them to varying degrees. We cultivate them to varying degrees.

Some talents need cultivating from a very early age or they can never develop fully.[2] Other abilities may not be discovered (or even needed) until much later in life.[3] No one is left out, though sadly, many natural talents and abilities may never be recognized or cultivated. In terms of development a lot depends upon the individual and the environment. However, both of these factors are under the direct influence of the Lord's grace and providential working. Doubtless, He helps us all discover and cultivate at least some of our innate abilities, even if we have no belief in Him. That too is His gift to us.

With conversion and the indwelling of the Holy Spirit, whole new attitudes arise within us. Even if we previously had been too timid or discouraged to discover our abilities or cultivate our known talents, all this is subject to change. A healthy prayer life and growing confidence in God, should be sufficient to help any believer recognize and cultivate their natural abilities above and beyond what they could have done without the Lord's help. Even so, it is important to realize that these are not yet what the Bible means by gifts. Any good thing a non-believer can do, you can do, too, if you have sufficient desire to cultivate that ability. Spiritual gifts are what only you can do and a non-believer cannot. Talents come to us through natural birth; gifts come to us through spiritual re-birth.

II. Good Fruit

There are three kinds of fruit that the Bible describes: the fruit of good deeds, the fruit of the Spirit and the fruit of Christian ministry. The first two can be cultivated by anyone on earth; only the third one can be cultivated by Christians.

1) The Fruit of Good Deeds. While it is definitely true that our good deeds alone can never be sufficient to save us, it is equally true that the Bible expects us to do good as much as we can, as well as we can and as often as we can.[4] You don't have to be a converted Christian to give to the poor, to work hard and honestly, to love your family or to defend your country. These are good things. We could call them "the fruit of righteousness" if that wouldn't give them too religious a cast.[5] No one needs faith in God to do them. However, just as with natural abilities, good deeds should flourish in the lives of genuine believers, since we can call on the Lord for help in cultivating them.

Turn away from evil and do good; seek peace and pursue it.
Psalms 34:11

2) The Fruit of the Spirit. These are fruit which can grow in our inner state: peace, love, joy, patience, kindness, goodness, faithfulness, gentleness and self-control.[6] All right thinking people everywhere prize these as feelings and praise them as virtues. Christians have a unique access to them through faith and grace, but we do not have exclusive receptivity to them for they are gifts of God to anyone who can receive them. Indeed, little children whose parents may be of any faith or of no faith, universally exhibit these fruit better than many of us who believe. As with natural abilities and good deeds, anyone can recognize, receive and cultivate this to a degree, but as believers we can enter into higher levels of these fruit[7] and learn the way of enhanced cultivation which Jesus desires.

Abide in me, and I in you. As the branch cannot bear fruit by itself, unless it abides in the vine, neither can you, unless you abide in me. I am the vine; you are the branches. Whoever abides in me and I in him, he it is that bears much fruit, for apart from me you can do nothing. John 15:4-5

3) The Fruit of Christian Ministry. In the widest sense Christian ministry includes anything that any believer might do as a service to others. However, you don't have to be a believer to spend your life in service to others. The New Testament letters generally narrow this category down into those specific things which we do for the sake of making Jesus known or for advancing His kingdom: such as preaching, praying, teaching, serving in His Name and doing healing, deliverance and miracles. This kind of fruit is a form of service unique to

Christians. It grows out of spiritual gifts that the Lord provides believers so that He can work in us and through us by His Spirit.

Now there are varieties of gifts, but the same Spirit; and there are varieties of service, but the same Lord; and there are varieties of activities, but it is the same God who empowers them all in everyone. 1 Corinthians 12:4-6

III. Gifts for Ministry

When we are reborn through the gift of faith and the indwelling of the Holy Spirit, the Lord showers fresh abilities and desires upon us. These are called "gifts and callings" and they go together like peas and carrots. Because of what the Lord plans to call us into doing, He gives us desires that inspire us and gifts that equip us for service in that direction. You can also count on it that once you discover any gifts or callings in you, they are there to stay. He doesn't revoke or withdraw them due to neglect, misuse or failed behavior.

For the gifts and the calling of God are irrevocable. Romans 11:29

There are three main kinds of spiritual gifts that we can receive, as well as others dropped in for good measure. These are commonly referred to as the five ministry gifts, the eight motivational gifts and the nine manifestation gifts. They will be discussed in the following three chapters. For now let's consider the difference between fruit and gifts, and specific gifts and general callings.

Fruit and Gifts

The good side of God's promise in Romans is that any effort we put into discovering our gifts and callings will always grow us towards our intended destiny: We can build on this as on a foundation that will never be removed. However, we need to build with wisdom. Character and integrity are entirely separate issues — they don't come with any of the gifts. They are fruit of the Spirit (for instance, faithfulness and self-control) that we must cultivate alongside of the gifts, otherwise we risk tarnishing the gifts, spreading confusion in the Body of Christ and giving the work a black eye to outsiders. Maybe someone's been given gifts of healing and evangelism, but if they steal from the offering and cheat on their spouse, that lack of character will bring their work to ruin. Don't let it happen to you!

Another difference between fruit and gifts is that fruit takes time to cultivate. Gifts can drop on you in an instant. The rule for fruit is that of natural cultivation: sow and grow. It takes a considerable amount of time to raise fruit trees to the point of harvesting a bumper crop. That should tell us something. We sow and grow by cultivating the 3 P's: prayer, patience and perseverance. As we die to the old ways of Self, the Holy Spirit raises us up into the ways of the Lord. That just doesn't happen overnight.

The rule with gifts is different: believe and receive. This calls for the 3 F's: faith, fact and feeling. By faith we trust ourselves to the facts in God's Word; then feelings follow as we receive what we ask or seek. Ask in faith for the gifts that your heart points you towards, believe in the fact of God's promise to gift and equip you, then step out into service and the feeling of being called and equipped will begin to show up. There's more to it than this, but that's enough to get anyone started.

Gifts and General Callings

Let's take it on faith for the moment that you have been given specific gifts and have a specific calling upon your life. Eventually, you will discover what these might be as you see what you like to do and what you do easily and well. Your friends may point some of this out to you, leaders may confirm it, and the Lord may reveal more through your hopes, dreams or encounters with Him. You have a unique purpose to fulfill and you have been exquisitely gifted to go at it. None of this, however, has anything to do with your general callings!

Every Christian knows Jesus by faith and has the Holy Spirit living inside of them. Therefore, every Christian has the potential of serving in any way that the Lord may ask of them from time to time. This has nothing to do with the way we may be best gifted and equipped to operate. It certainly has nothing to do with our comfort zones or personal desires. Just because I may not be called and gifted to be an evangelist, doesn't exclude me from the call of God to share my faith in Christ. I may not have any discernible gifts of healing, but I am still called to pray for the sick. You may not be a pastor, but you still will need to know how to comfort, encourage and guide your friends and others the Lord may put in your path.

These general callings of God are in the scriptures and they are directed to all of us. Sure some have champion level gifts, but all of us are soldiers and may be required to step into any role at a moment's notice. This can easily seem intimidating at first (and at times along the way), because it means that God may ask us to step out of our comfort zone and rely on Him to help us fill in when no one better equipped in standing by. The beautiful side of this is that nothing is excluded from us: We can grow in every direction to some degree and we can, therefore, reap the blessing of experiencing that part of the Rescue.

CHAPTER 18

FIVE MINISTRY GIFTS

Everyone benefits directly from these five gifts for they are given by the Father for the express purpose of building up the whole Body of Christ so that we can be fully equipped to play our part in the Rescue. Considering how important they are in God's plan, it should not be too surprising that the enemy has tried to eliminate or decimate them. Several of these ministry gifts have nearly passed out of everyday experience for many in the church. The good news is that they are all staging a comeback!

And he gave the apostles, the prophets, the evangelists, the pastors and teachers, to equip the saints for the work of ministry, for building up the body of Christ, until we all attain to the unity of the faith and of the knowledge of the Son of God, to mature manhood, to the measure of the stature of the fullness of Christ. Ephesians 4:11-13

Centuries of Neglect

Looking at church history through the lens of the above passage from Ephesians, it's fair to say that for centuries, perhaps as many as 18, the primary office of leadership in the church has been that of pastor. Whether Protestant or Catholic, Orthodox or Independent, the pastor, minister, preacher or priest is the focal point for the local congregation's experience of leadership in the church. True enough there may be bishops or superintendents above the local pastor and elders alongside, but where are the other offices? Paul is unambiguous that in the church there are meant to be "apostles, prophets, evangelists and teachers" as well as pastors. What happened?

The legalization and expansion of the early church in the fourth century of the Roman Empire watered down the depth of experience for most Christians from the time of Constantine the Great onwards. As persecution no longer drove the church underground and deeper into Christ, being a Christian became socially acceptable, even preferable.[1] Genuine conversions were no longer the expected norm—they were replaced by infant baptism—and the gifts of the Spirit largely disappeared. At the same time the administrative structure of the church increasingly mirrored that of the Empire with its leaders holding offices of administrative power. This process actually had begun just over a century earlier as bishops won out over the charismatically gifted for leadership over the church.[2]

These developments were probably necessary for establishing stable order within the church—there was so much naiveté and credulity in those days. However, two of the biggest losers during this season of growth and transformation were the baptism in the Holy Spirit and the gifts of the Spirit. Perhaps this was inevitable. It may have been by the Lord's doing that these aspects of His power had to await a time when the church as a whole would be in a better position to handle them. What's clear is that they were never intended to disappear entirely or stay submerged indefinitely. Throughout history the miraculous continued to dazzle here and there like jewels in a river bed. Then, in the last century a stunning resurrection has brought these lost treasures to the surface.

A Century of Renewal

Just as the Catholic Middle Ages proved to be a period of incubation for those ideas which burst forth in the Reformation, so, too, the Pentecostal and Charismatic moments of the twentieth century owed their emergence to the prayer and piety which grew in the intervening centuries of Protestant Orthodoxy. People were hungering for a deeper, more authentic experience of both the passion and power of the Early Church. Where the Protestant Reformation focused on the Person of Jesus and His saving work, the Pentecostal revival turned its sights towards the Person of the Holy Spirit and His supernatural gifts.

This combination was explosive: The Welch Revival and that of Azusa Street quickly brought the baptism in the Spirit and His supernatural workings to millions worldwide. Revivals and outpourings have continued to break forth, as have the baptism in the Spirit and its controversial sign—speaking in tongues. Despite opposition from mainline Christianity, the movement has spread, becoming the fastest growing and third largest branch of Christianity.

In addition there have been revivals led by extraordinarily gifted healers, prophets with Biblical levels of supernatural vision and accuracy, teachers who have gained universal recognition for their gifts, and evangelists who have reached millions even in single events. Miracles of healing and demonic deliverance have become "the children's bread" once again in the life of many churches, especially those in the Third World.[3] Once birthed these gifts and callings have continued to grow in depth of understanding and breadth of expansion. There has been no turning back! In one wave after another it is evident that a Mighty Hand has been restoring gifts to His Son's Bride which were never intended to languish unopened.

The Body of Christ in the twenty first century is, therefore, entering a restored season of all the elements of supernatural giftedness that the Early Church once enjoyed. No doubt many things are still in a process of growth towards full restoration, but the main pieces are on the drawing room table. Now is the time for seeing how they will fit together in preparation for the extensive growth that will very likely come as a result. Sadly, some will miss out, blinded by doctrines that keep them from seeing what the Lord is doing in our day. That needn't be you!

The Fivefold Ministry

The entry point for all of us into this dimension of Christian living is the baptism in the Spirit. With it come praying in tongues and access to at least some of the nine supernatural gifts. The fivefold ministry is there (when it is there) to help all believers cultivate their gifts and find their place in the Body as fellow ministers, but it is especially needed by those who have been baptized in the Holy Spirit. Why? Why isn't the traditional pattern of the pastor/teacher sufficient?

Pastors are usually perfectly able to equip believers to serve on the governing board, to teach in Sunday school, to be ushers, or lead home groups, visit the sick at hospital, or canvass the neighborhood in outreach and evangelism. That's a lot. But you don't have to be baptized in the Spirit or supernaturally gifted to do any of it! And neither does the pastor. In the spiritual life it is practically impossible to lead or cultivate others beyond your own level of experience. In the Biblical pattern all of the fivefold ministers were already baptized in the Spirit and operating in their gifts as part of a team. This positioned them powerfully for equipping others to join in the effort of a supernaturally gifted Body to do the kinds of ministry which only Holy Spirit empowered Christians can do. Look where Paul places the priority in leadership: apostles first, then prophets. Pastors are not even mentioned.[4]

Now you are the body of Christ and individually members of it. And God has appointed in the church first apostles, second prophets, third teachers, then miracles, then gifts of healing, helping, administrating, and various kinds of tongues. 1 Corinthians 12:27-28

Without question, the New Testament apostles were Holy Spirit baptized and equipped for supernatural ministry.[5] So were the prophets. So were many, if not all, of the others in leadership positions, judging by the above list which includes supernatural gifts. Furthermore, the apostles were frequently tasked with rounding up the believers that hadn't yet been baptized in the Holy Spirit and laying hands on them until they were.[6] It would appear that the Early Church was so universally charismatic that those who weren't stood out as exceptions to be further instructed.[7] Just as the members of the Early Church could look with confidence to their leaders, recognizing the gifts of those the Lord had placed over them, so we need to understand these gifts for the sake of our own equipping. Seeing the head will help us find our place in the Body.[8]

1) Apostles. After Jesus' resurrection the twelve disciples He had chosen became the principal apostles and the uncontested leaders of the Early Church.[9] Paul's apostolic position was later recognized by these men, but was contested by others who sought to gain influence over churches he had established. Others were added to the ranks of the apostles, though the number of "false apostles" evidently increased as well.[10] Additionally, the Early Church recognized a distinction between apostles who held universal authority in the church and elders who functioned as local administrators or as advisers to the apostles.[11] We should expect it then that as this office is restored to the church controversy will likely surround it. How to recognize true apostles?

The first apostles knew the Lord personally and well. They had learned directly from Him and had seen Him resurrected in power. Their faith and their knowledge of God was, therefore, both intimate and authoritative for others who wanted to be taught by them. This will be one of the marks. Another is the way they shepherded the growth and missionary spread of the Early Church. They had a genuine vision for the harvest of souls and church planting. A third indicator was their ability to move in supernatural power. Paul said he demonstrated all of the signs of a true apostle.[12] Perhaps, the greatest mark of a true apostle, however, will be the way the other four offices recognize the apostle's God-given authority and submit their ministries to apostolic oversight.

2) Prophets. Prophets abound in both Testaments of the Bible. The unmistakable mark of a true prophet is Holy Spirit given insight and foresight. They are able to see things that others don't or can't. They can foretell future events through dreams or visions they receive from the Lord (foresight). They can also "read" the innermost secrets of a person through whatever unique way the Lord chooses to work through them (insight).[13] In addition to foretelling, prophets were called to "forth tell"—to speak forth the counsel of God's holy standard against sin, calling the people to repentance.

With the New Covenant there is no less emphasis upon holy living, but a much greater emphasis upon the grace of God to accomplish it. Accordingly, there is a marked difference in temperament between the way Old and New Testament prophets present their messages. Whereas OT prophets seemed to thunder at the people from on high, inveighing against them, New Testament prophets encourage and enlighten the people from below as loving servants.[14] Consider the difference in tone between Moses at Sinai or Elijah at Mount Carmel and Jesus, who is the greatest of all prophets, giving the Sermon on the Mount. Give special respect to those prophets who not only have supernatural gifts from the Holy Spirit, but show forth the nature of Jesus in the way they minister to others.

3) Evangelists. Even under the Old Covenant it was expected that Abraham's offspring would carry the "good news" about their God to the outside world.[15] This happened to a limited degree during the Jewish Diaspora as god-fearers were attracted to the Synagogues which sprang up throughout the Mediterranean basin. The Early Church carried this to a whole new level with a brand new message.

Both Stephen, the first martyr, and Philip displayed awesome gifts of evangelism. Soon, practically everyone everywhere was hearing the message.[16] Nowadays, we are all familiar with this gift, especially after the explosion of converts taking place through the ministries of men like Billy Graham and Reinhard Bonnke. Nevertheless, evangelists aren't always on platforms or in the mission field. Look for them in the local church, too.

4) Pastors. Pastors are shepherds of the flock. This is the office most familiar to all of us, so there is little need to delineate it here. It is modeled quite naturally on Jesus as our ultimate Good Shepherd who (in the gospels) cared for and cultivated the faith of lost individuals, the inner circle of devout followers and the wider gatherings of interested, though somewhat less committed believers. Typically, pastors are the head of the local church and as such, everyone needs to submit to their authority, even those who might consider that they have a higher gift and calling.

Being the head pastor, however, doesn't mean that pastoring is their gift, only their position with its common title. Many pastors are gifted as evangelists or teachers with little God-given ability to do actual pastoring. That's not their fault—it may be ours for expecting them to be all things for all people, when the Lord told us in advance that He gives out five different kinds of leadership gifts for equipping us.

5) Teachers. For centuries the academic model dominated this gift. The great Luther was himself a seminary professor, though there was certainly nothing stale or pedantic about his preaching. Nevertheless, with their renewed emphasis upon the Word of God, many Protestant churches sometimes seemed designed to resemble lecture halls with sermons given like a scholarly address. This approach has perhaps had the unfortunate effect of cultivating head knowledge at the expense of practical experience and personal transformation. In the closing decades of the last century a new kind of teacher emerged out of the charismatic movement. These are being recognized across denominational lines for the power of their gift to open the scriptures in such a way that "our hearts burned with us" once again.[17]

You may not find a church with all five of these offices filled. That's not the main thing you need, so don't let it disturb you. The main thing is seeking to be faithful to what Jesus would have you do. Let Him place you where He wills and lead you as He desires. In any healthy church you will certainly find leaders who will gladly help you get started ministering with the gifts they discern in you.

CHAPTER 19

SEVEN MOTIVATIONAL GIFTS

These should be of particular interest to everyone, since each of us has been given at least one. Oddly enough, it's not always obvious to us what our unique gift is. Perhaps the Lord enjoys playing Hide and Seek more than we might imagine. Here's a clue: Usually you will find them hidden in plain sight, since people often live out of their gift before they catch on to what it is. Intrigued? See if you can spot your own.

> **Having gifts that differ according to the grace given to us, let us use them: if prophecy, in proportion to our faith; if service, in our serving; the one who teaches, in his teaching; the one who exhorts, in his exhortation; the one who contributes, in generosity; the one who leads, with zeal; the one who does acts of mercy, with cheerfulness.**
> Romans 12:6-8

Supernaturally Natural

These seven gifts are called motivational gifts because they provide the inner focus that inspires us to get into the game of serving humanity in our own particular way. We have an inner drive or motivation that causes us to notice certain areas of need in the church or the world and then keeps us looking for ways of meeting that need. All of this happens to match our gift so "naturally" that we may never stop to question or examine it. We might wonder, "Why doesn't everyone feel this way?" and be genuinely surprised that they don't.

Having one of these gifts doesn't mean that we are going to be great at it automatically. They have to be cultivated like anything else in life. And they won't work very well if we aren't in balance with the Lord (more on that later). Nevertheless, the sense of inner compelling is so consistent and so intimately tied into our own desires that it practically guarantees that we will develop real skills to go along with the gift. If we don't, it won't be for lack of effort, since the gift keeps pointing us at the same target over and over again. This inner motivation is nothing less than God at work within us "for his good pleasure."[1]

> **Therefore, my beloved, as you have always obeyed, so now, not only as in my presence but much more in my absence, work out your own salvation with fear and trembling, for it is God who works in you, both to will and to work for his good pleasure.** Philippians 2:12-13

This means that there will be joy in it, because God is working in us to make us willing (desirous) of doing what He is also enabling us to do. It "pleases" the Lord to work through us and He is very good about passing His feelings on to us. This doesn't mean that we can't ever burn out the inner flame. We can. It feels so good operating out of our gift that exhausting ourselves is a danger that has to be guarded against. However, the Lord always stands ready to renew and refresh us. If we allow Him to do that—wonder of wonders—the former desires have a way of springing right back to life! This inner drive comes from His holy fire to burn brightly within us in this particular way and that flame can never be quenched.

> **For God's gifts and His call are irrevocable. [He never withdraws them when once they are given, and He does not change His mind about those to whom He gives His grace or to whom He sends His call.]** Romans 11:29 AMP

Primary and Secondary

As you look over the list you may notice right away the gift that is your primary motivation. If you can't spot it, others who know you well probably can. The Holy Spirit has been cultivating these inner motivations in us since childhood in terms of general orientation.[2] Conversion and the entrance of the Holy Spirit within us may bring new aspects and abilities out to the forefront, as well as unveil for us new applications within the Christian community. For instance someone gifted as a teacher may have been growing happily in that area all their life, but conversion will likely bring whole new levels of purpose and initiate a brand new desire to teach spiritual truths.

Some confusion may arise over just how many gifts you have. Paul gives us little to go on beyond the mere recounting of the list. There is nothing here to limit these to one per person. You could conceivably have several primary gifts and rotate though times of being more focused on one rather than the other. Nevertheless, the common pattern is for a person to have a single primary gift with one or more secondary gifts that complement and enhance its operation. In this way the Lord provides a natural sense of cohesion and wholeness to our inner focus and motivation: We aren't as likely to be pulled in three directions at once! Even so, all of us can (and probably should) cultivate each of these gifts to some degree.

Flesh Verses Spirit

Since these gifts are the Holy Spirit working within us, we might suppose that our gift(s) will always work for good in our life and for the good of those we seek to serve. Not so! It is too much to be hoped that these inner workings of the Lord cannot be subverted by the enemy. Spiritual darkness loves to turn even good things against us. As mentioned earlier, if we don't stay in balance these gifts of His won't operate properly. The key to staying balanced is living with Jesus at the center and with ourselves surrendered and submitted to His leadership. He hasn't given us gifts and callings so that we can go charging off on our own.

As with anything in this new life in Christ, our actual trust in the Lord determines practically everything else. If you want to serve Him and others, if you want your gift(s) to be operating at peak performance, then you will want to learn to guard your heart so that the peace of Christ rules within you.[3] There is no clearer indication that we are yielded to His leadership than the peace He gives us when we are trusting Him and doing things His way.[4] With that peace in place the motivational gifts positively hum! It is truly amazing, even breathtaking to be flowing in these gifts. This is part of what it means to be led by the Spirit.[5]

We can, however, fall back into being oppressed by the flesh.[6] It is easy and "natural" to fall out of the Spirit and into the flesh, even when we are trying to serve the Lord. Because the flesh is our fallen nature, falling into it almost feels normal. The absence of the peace of Christ should alert us that something has gone wrong. That wrongness will inevitably show up by distorting the gifts we cherish and enjoy, turning service into something onerous, rather than delightful. In the following brief descriptions note how being in "the flesh" can distort the gift. Note also the wonderful purpose the gift can serve when we are in the Spirit.

For we are his workmanship, created in Christ Jesus for good works, which God prepared beforehand, that we should walk in them.
Ephesians 2:10

Seven Motivational Gifts

Because it is possible for believers to receive the indwelling Spirit, but never seek or receive the baptism in the Spirit, there will be differences in the way these gifts operate in those who are not Holy Spirit baptized. Remember, the Early Church that Paul shepherded was almost entirely composed of people who had received the baptism in the Spirit. Hence, he would have had in his mind the way these gifts look in the lives of people who know Jesus by faith and are also anointed with the Spirit's power.

1) Prophesying: "If prophecy, in proportion to our faith." People with this gift usually know it and are eager to cultivate it, because it often brings enhanced opportunities to experience the supernatural workings of the Holy Spirit. Prophets have a burning heart for receiving specific words or visions from God which will bring clarity to individuals or churches. Clarity comes by calling people to repentance, pointing out their sin; or through sharing visions, restoring lost spiritual sight. If those with the gift of prophecy have not yet received the baptism in the Spirit, their emphasis will be more on the Word of God, than specific words *from* God. If in the flesh, people with this gift may lose the New Testament tone of grace, becoming hard and judgmental, ministering the law's condemnation, rather than the gospel's love and mercy.

2) Serving: "If service, in our serving." The Amplified Bible calls this "practical service." That's the proper note. The person with this gift is always noticing things of a practical nature that will help an individual or the church, and then throwing themselves into the fray to get the job done. It's been said that love is an active verb; certainly these are the ones who put feet to their prayers. That is if they haven't slipped into the flesh. The danger here is leaping, before praying, and thereby taking the lead away from the Lord. This can lead to misguided efforts, feeling unappreciated or burn out, if left to the flesh. Pastors always appreciate the gift of service (not necessarily that of prophesy!) and they can and should help these good hearted workers learn the ways of wisdom. If this is your gift, try to remember that seeing a need isn't always a call of God for personal action; it may be a call to prayer instead.

3) Teaching: "The one who teaches, in his teaching." A teacher's focus is different than a prophet's in that their concern is more for the whole counsel of the Word of God with a willingness to leave the individual's response to conscience. Prophets are more inclined to "zero in" on specifics and seek to close the deal. In our day a great line is drawn between preaching and teaching, but not in the Bible. Jesus' "preaching" was called teaching and so was that of the apostles—it's one of the main things they were known for.[7] Teachers with an anointing will teach truth in order to elicit the saving transformation they know that particular truth can bring. Teachers in the flesh are focused upon get the head knowledge right, filling minds with information, while leaving hearts empty and thirsting.

4) Exhorting: "The one who exhorts, in his exhortation." Exhortation is better known to us as encouragement, a word which means to give courage to the hearts of others. Exhorters are always looking for opportunities to do that. Who is cast down? Who needs building up? How can their spirits be lifted higher? Where a teacher wants to help you learn truths you don't know yet, an exhorter wants to help you believe what you already know. Notice how this plays out with different preaching styles:

Some preachers are teachers at heart; others are exhorters. Meanwhile, some of the best exhorters don't have a public ministry. They just naturally lift the mood of individuals wherever they go. Watch out for one in the flesh, however, if you don't want to find out firsthand what the "gift of discouragement" looks like in operation.

5) Giving: "The one who contributes, in generosity." The Lord evidently calls some people to gather wealth, so that through them, He can bless others and the church. It's a tough job, but someone has to do it. The thing about these folks is their absence of greed and the evident delight they have in giving money or material help away. They usually seem consciously aware that their calling is to be a channel of blessing and they genuinely want to keep the river flowing. If they fall into the flesh, all bets are off: They may amass wealth for themselves alone, or seek a show of recognition for what they do give away.

6) Leading: "The one who leads, with zeal." The gift of administration includes the ability to supervise others, cast vision, assemble a team and chart a course all with unflagging "zeal" or diligence. If this is your gift, then know that the rest of us are grateful you have it! We need your energetic devotion to duty or things would really fall apart. We thank God for your integrity and willingness to sacrifice ordinary pleasures for the sake of the cause. Just please don't "lord" it over us, bossing us around! Jesus said that our leaders would be servants to us and those with this gift truly are—whenever they are in the Spirit. Otherwise…

7) Caring: "The one who does acts of mercy, with cheerfulness." Last, but not least, is the heart of the Body of Christ. People blessed with a mercy gift have hearts as big and warm as your mama's stove. They notice the hurting people among us and launch into prayer, then press in to draw them out. They care less about how you got into trouble, than how to get you out. Unlike teachers and prophets, they don't want to know if you are learning from the experience; they want you free of the pain.

These are people you can trust with your heart. Unfortunately, when in the flesh, their own heart can take them down, if they don't learn how to cast every care and all that pain on the Lord.

Put it all together and you have a vision for the Body of Christ as a mighty warrior, able to tend its own wounds and refresh its own vision when all the parts are working together as designed. Discover your gift, learn how to walk in the Spirit with it, and find your place in the Body!

Holy Spirit

CHAPTER 20

NINE GIFTS OF POWER

Jesus never intended for His church to be powerless or penniless. Just as the tithe is the Lord's provision for material supply, so the baptism in the Spirit is His provision for supernatural supply. Neither is forced on anyone, but when believers come into obedience, watch out—the windows of heaven open wide![1] Through the baptism in the Spirit, Jesus pours out gifts that will manifest as signs and wonders for the sake of ministry to someone He wants to bless.

To each is given the manifestation of the Spirit for the common good.
1 Corinthians 12:7

A Context for Understanding

The main passage concerning the nine gifts of supernatural power is Paul's account in 1 Corinthians 12:1-12 where they are set within a wider context. Since he was writing to a church that was experiencing these gifts and was already familiar with how they worked, Paul doesn't take time to describe them.[2] That's a pity for us, because many of us grew up in churches devoid of these supernatural operations.

Experience is the best teacher when it is available; absence of experience gives false ideas plenty of room to grow. Nevertheless, we can surmise what these gifts would have looked like then, by their appearances in other passages of scripture and by the way they are breaking forth in Charismatic and Pentecostal churches where the baptism of the Spirit is flourishing today. Before we examine the individual gifts, let's look at the context Paul gave them.

Now concerning spiritual gifts, brothers, I do not want you to be uninformed. 1 Corinthians 12:1

According to St. Paul, the very first thing that we need to know concerning spiritual gifts is to avoid being "uninformed." Learning about something is usually the first step towards doing it, but it is also a necessary step towards allowing others to do a thing. Why does that matter? In western churches many people have pulled away from the supernatural operations of the Holy Spirit due to fear and false teaching. By being uninformed of the truth, they not only aren't seeking to make themselves available for God to work through them, they are actively hindering others from going forward.

> **Now there are varieties of gifts, but the same Spirit; and there are varieties of service, but the same Lord; and there are varieties of activities, but it is the same God who empowers them all in everyone. To each is given the manifestation of the Spirit for the common good.** 1 Corinthians 12:4-7

The whole of the Trinity is involved in the operation of these gifts: the Holy Spirit who works through the gift we are given, the Lord Jesus whose church is being served by the gift, and God the Father who oversees it all for the sake of everyone involved. Elsewhere Paul will describe other gifts and their place in the Body of Christ.[3] Here his concern is only for certain gifts he now calls "manifestations of the Spirit." Whatever is "manifest" has been brought to the light. It is something obvious and evident. These are gifts which make it obvious that God is at work through them. They display supernatural power in a way that the other gifts do not.

> **All these are empowered by one and the same Spirit, who apportions to each one individually as he wills. For just as the body is one and has many members, and all the members of the body, though many, are one body, so it is with Christ.** 1 Corinthians 12:1-12

Because these gifts are manifestations of the Spirit, it is God alone who "apportions"—who chooses who, when and where. Although these "activities" can be counterfeited by the enemy, the operation of the true gifts is entirely under the Holy Spirit's control. They can't be worked up by human effort. This is an important point for discerning how these gifts differ from normal human abilities. For instance, anyone who teaches can convey intellectual knowledge about a subject, but that is not what is meant by the "word of knowledge." We look to doctors for healing, but their gifts are not "gifts of healings." Certainly, God may work through doctors and teachers (let's hope He does!), but His work is hidden, not manifest, except in outcome. These nine gifts manifest *during* the process of ministering to others.

The Nine Gifts of Power

For to one is given the word of wisdom through the Spirit, to another the word of knowledge through the same Spirit, to another faith by the same Spirit, to another gifts of healings by the same Spirit, to another the working of miracles, to another prophecy, to another discerning of spirits, to another different kinds of tongues, to another the interpretation of tongues. 1 Corinthians 12:8-10 NKJV

1) **"The word of wisdom."** Wisdom is available to everyone who asks for it or seeks it.[4] The whole of Proverbs, for instance, is devoted to helping us gain practical wisdom and understanding for daily living. This accumulation of good sense and insight is akin to, but not exactly, what is meant by "the word of wisdom."

Solomon's most famous judgment gives us an example of this gift in operation. Having previously prayed for wisdom, God gave Solomon the perfect solution to a troubling dilemma: Which prostitute was the true mother of the child who died and which was lying. Solomon's decision in the case revealed to all Israel that that God was with him, giving wisdom.

Then the king answered and said, "Give the living child to the first woman, and by no means put him to death; she is his mother." And all Israel heard of the judgment that the king had rendered, and they stood in awe of the king, because they perceived that the wisdom of God was in him to do justice. 1 Kings 3:27-28

2) **"The word of knowledge."** This gift has a very strong prophetic component, giving "knowledge" to both the one who receives it and the one being ministered to that God is at work in a given situation. This elevates the faith level of everyone present for whatever it is that the Lord desires to do. Often, however, it doesn't seem like a word at all. In the context of a healing service

it may be a sense of pain felt by the prayer minister in a very specific part of their body.

When that "word" is spoken out ("Someone here has ringing in their left ear that God wants to heal"), a person in the congregation with that condition will usually experience increased faith, often receiving healing as a direct result. When the blind man was told Jesus wanted to see him, his faith level was certainly enhanced. Jesus saw his response, noted the faith, and the healing happened.

> And Jesus stopped and said, "Call him." And they called the blind man, saying to him, "Take heart. Get up; he is calling you." And throwing off his cloak, he sprang up and came to Jesus. And Jesus said to him, "What do you want me to do for you?" And the blind man said to him, "Rabbi, let me recover my sight." And Jesus said to him, "Go your way; your faith has made you well." And immediately he recovered his sight and followed him on the way. Mark 10:49-52

3) "Faith." All who believe in Jesus have already received the gift of faith, so saving faith or faith in Christ's death and resurrection is not what is meant by this gift.[5] This gift conveys a supernaturally sustained ability to trust God in a specific situation or to believe for a specific purpose or activity that the Lord wants to accomplish. Persons who receive it don't have to work at believing God against what may seem like impossible odds.[6] They only have to make sure they don't lose what they have received.

Often this ability to believe with heightened faith is activated by a specific word "quickened" from scripture or received directly from the Spirit. David's confident faith for killing Goliath seems to have been sustained by this kind of gift.

> And David said, "The Lord who delivered me from the paw of the lion and from the paw of the bear will deliver me from the hand of this Philistine." And Saul said to David, "Go, and the Lord be with you!" 1 Samuel 17:37

4) "Gifts of healings." There are so many things about us that can go wrong: physical sickness, systemic disease, organ failure, accidental injury, mental disease, and emotional wounds. It's no wonder that many "gifts" for "healings" are needed.

Everyone should pray for healing, all of us can seek to receive a greater capacity for effective prayer, but certain individuals have already been unquestionably gifted by the Lord for healing. Many of them are consciously aware of an anointing from the Lord which "signals" His presence upon them to heal someone. Sometimes it is a sensation of physical warmth on their hands; at other times it may be an ability to "see" faith upon someone, as with Paul in Lystra.

> **And in Lystra a certain man without strength in his feet was sitting, a cripple from his mother's womb, who had never walked. This man heard Paul speaking. Paul, observing him intently and seeing that he had faith to be healed, said with a loud voice, "Stand up straight on your feet!" And he leaped and walked.**
> Acts 14:8-11 NKJV

5) "The working of miracles." Of course, sudden healings are miracles in themselves, but what is (likely) intended here are those activities of God which affect the natural order, not the human body—what are usually termed "signs and wonders" in the Hebrew scriptures.[7] Nature, too, can go awry. Jesus rebuked the wind for His disciples' sake. God stopped the mouths of lions for Daniel's sake. He also brought forth water from a rock and provided *mana* in the wilderness for His chosen people.

We, too, need miracles of all kinds in our lives: miracles of escape from imminent danger or looming debt; miracles of provision; miracles of deadly forces in nature stopped or turned aside. We have an awesome God-given ability to "speak" even to mountains, commanding nature just as Jesus did.

> **And he said to it, "May no fruit ever come from you again!" And the fig tree withered at once. When the disciples saw it, they marveled, saying, "How did the fig tree wither at once?" And Jesus answered them, "Truly, I say to you, if you have faith and do not doubt, you will not only do what has been done to the fig tree, but**

even if you say to this mountain, 'Be taken up and thrown into the sea,' it will happen." Matthew 21:19-21

6) "Prophecy." There are many levels to the prophetic. At the entry level is the kind of seeking we all do in prayer to find a word of encouragement or just the right book from an inspired author to match a friend's need. Jesus says that all of His sheep "hear" His voice. Some do more than others.

Those with a prophetic gift hear more frequently and more specifically from the Lord by means of a "language" of prophetic communication that may include dreams, visions, symbols and pictures, even more than words. This does not mean they get it right all of the time, but that they develop a dependable track record for accuracy which makes it worthwhile for others to pay attention to, weigh, and sift their sayings. Agabus' prophetic gift helped the church prepare for a famine.

Now in these days prophets came down from Jerusalem to Antioch. And one of them named Agabus stood up and foretold by the Spirit that there would be a great famine over all the world (this took place in the days of Claudius). So the disciples determined, everyone according to his ability, to send relief to the brothers living in Judea. Acts 11:27-29

7) "Discerning of spirits." Having been active in the field of demonic deliverance, I can testify that there are at least two levels to the operation of this gift. There are some people (myself at times) who can discern by inward sense which demon needs to be cast out of a person, which spirits are oppressing a church or other organization, and even where angels or demons may be positioned around a room. There are others who have been given sight to see into the invisible realm that surrounds us all.

I have worked with many people who evidently had this ability, whose credibility and Christian character gave support to what they reported seeing. In battlefield conditions having someone with this gift is like having a spy behind enemy lines. To Balaam's chagrin, however, his donkey saw the angel before he did. Nevertheless, it was a good thing he listened to what the donkey discerned.

And the donkey said to Balaam, "Am I not your donkey, on which you have ridden all your life long to this day? Is it my habit to treat you this way?" And he said, "No." Then the Lord opened the eyes of Balaam, and he saw the angel of the Lord standing in the way, with his drawn sword in his hand. And he bowed down and fell on his face. Numbers 22:30-31

8) "Different kinds of tongues." In addition to "tongues" or languages that can be learned by the usual human means, there are tongues "of men and of angels" which are given by God for His own specific purposes.[8] On the day of Pentecost everyone in the Upper Room was baptized in the Holy Spirit and given an ability to speak human languages that they could not have previously known. This was a sign to the multitudes who heard them "speaking in their own tongue"—a convincing display of God's power which led to Peter's sermon and the conversion of 3000.[9]

There are also "tongues of angels" by which the Lord may be worshiped or entreated. These tongues have no human counterpart. The tongues spoken of here may be of either variety, but the setting is public worship, which is why it is stipulated that an interpretation should be given, something that is completely unnecessary if they are simply a part of the person's private prayer language. Such a setting requires interpretation for the sake of proclaiming the prophecy it contains.

Now I want you all to speak in tongues, but even more to prophesy. The one who prophesies is greater than the one who speaks in tongues, unless someone interprets, so that the church may be built up... So with yourselves, since you are eager for manifestations of the Spirit, strive to excel in building up the church. 1 Corinthians 14:5, 12

9) "The interpretation of tongues." Interpreting tongues which are publicly uttered is necessary for the Lord to accomplish what the tongues describe. Without the interpretation coming forth, no one knows what was said. No one can even be confident that the tongues conveyed a message from the Lord or

129

were initiated by Him, rather than from of the speaker's own soul.

This gets tricky really fast because the speaker has to have faith that someone is present who will be able to interpret what he/she believes God has prompted them to say (perhaps that will be themselves); likewise the interpreter has to have faith to believe that they are hearing from God at least enough of the message to launch out in faith to let it flow in fullness.[10]

Therefore, one who speaks in a tongue should pray for the power to interpret. 1 Corinthians 14:13

Learning about these gifts is not the same thing as doing them, but it is a necessary beginning. To go further you will need a fellowship of like-minded believers who are committed to discovering how to make themselves available to God, Jesus and the Holy Spirit at this level. You can be sure that there are others who are pursuing these things of God, as well as the Lord Himself. Passion for Jesus and compassion for others will carry anyone a long way towards the unfolding of every gift the Holy Spirit desires to release through us—if we don't set preconceived limits to what is possible. You can be sure that the Lord doesn't!

CHAPTER 21

DOING MINISTRY

There's nothing like doing the thing, especially when what we are doing is something we can be sure that Jesus is doing right along with us. The real Minister, the true Servant, is there on the inside wanting to get out into that hurting, lost world through us His chosen vessels. The secret to kingdom success is letting Him do ministry through you. It is also the secret to never becoming burned out.

For it is God who works in you, both to will and to work for his good pleasure. Philippians 2:13

Our Secret of Success

Success in ministry is learning to let Jesus work in you and through you. We need to let Him work in us so that He can work through us. On good days this can be as easy as child's play. When our trust, love and inward surrender are high, we hardly need any coaching from a book like this. We're good to go! At other times, however, it is as tough as nails. Why is that?

Because Jesus is in you, the Holy Spirit will lift and lead you into the many joys of working with Him, making you feel childlike and free.[1] Likewise, precisely because Jesus is in you, the enemy's camp will work steadily to oppose anything He might want to do through you. At those times you will feel hindered and besieged. Remember, too, that the Adversary doesn't just come at us from the outside; difficulties also arise from all that is still fallen within us. That's why we have to learn to let Jesus work *in* us, in order for Him to keep working through us.

There is no escaping this ongoing conflict. Just be ready for it. It is the inevitable cycle of our new life: struggle and victory, seed time and harvest, death to Self and resurrection with Christ.[2] Be encouraged: Opposition from the enemy is never wasted. God will always overturn it and use it to advance His work. In addition it often serves as the Lord's wash and wear cycle—something that He puts us through whenever we need to be cleansed of Self and liberated once again as glad-hearted, unencumbered children.[3]

We need this friendly work of the Lord in us because it is so easy to get caught up in trying to get results. Our desire to help people can easily be subverted by the enemy. We could focus on the problems and lose the peace of Christ, then press forward in our own strength until we've burned out the inner flame. Or, we might seize the reigns, trying to manage everything according to our own understanding and our own sense of timing. This always leads to frustration. Without even realizing it, by these and other ways we can take control of the work away from the Lord into our own hands. This never produces the desired results!

Success in ministry is letting Jesus have His way with us. His top priority is growing loving relationships—that's the key result He's looking for. Are we making the progress there that He desires? As for the work itself, it always goes better if Jesus is in the lead. He alone knows what He desires to accomplish and how to do it. The great thing about this is that He can be immensely pleased even with what may seem to us like miniscule gains, such as stopping what you're doing to give "a cup of water" to someone in need.[4]

Learning to follow Him is filled with unexpected moments of purpose and accomplishment when something vital (love, empathy, shared understanding) passes between us and the people we serve. Our service is also marked by times of quandary: Where did He go now? What was that about? What is He trying to teach me? Since so much depends upon Jesus doing His ministry through us, we need to understand and cooperate with this dynamic of the work.

The Source of Our Success

Jesus gathered the disciples on His last night with them for a final teaching on how to do ministry once He was gone. Just as they had always done ministry under His leadership while He was with them in the flesh, so now they were to make sure that He remained in charge once He was gone. But catch the wink: He wouldn't really be gone. He would remain with them as an abiding presence and He fully expected them (and us) to learn how to return the favor by learning to abide in Him. This teaching is so important that we need to study it in detail.

> Abide in me, and I in you. As the branch cannot bear fruit by itself, unless it abides in the vine, neither can you, unless you abide in me. I am the vine; you are the branches. Whoever abides in me and I in him, he it is that bears much fruit, for apart from me you can do nothing. If anyone does not abide in me he is thrown away like a branch and withers; and the branches are gathered, thrown into the fire, and burned. If you abide in me, and my words abide in you, ask whatever you wish, and it will be done for you. By this my Father is glorified, that you bear much fruit and so prove to be my disciples. As the Father has loved me, so have I loved you. Abide in my love. If you keep my commandments, you will abide in my love, just as I have kept my Father's commandments and abide in his love. These things I have spoken to you, that my joy may be in you, and that your joy may be full... You did not choose me, but I chose you and appointed you that you should go and bear fruit and that your fruit should abide, so that whatever you ask the Father in my name, he may give it to you.
> John 15:4-11, 16

Our abiding is important to Jesus, as well as the fruit we are intended to bear. Unless we learn the way of abiding in Him we will be unable to bear *any* fruit. On the other hand, if we abide in Him, we will bear "much fruit." Bearing fruit glorifies the Father and proves that we are truly His disciples. The stakes are high! If we don't learn to abide in Him, we not only won't experience the overflow of His joy, we may actually risk being cast "into the fire." Indeed, we have been chosen that we "should go and bear fruit."

Fruit is what the branch (that's us) produces by abiding in the vine (that's Jesus). Fruit is not for the consumption of the branch, but for the nourishment of others. In the New Testament there are three basic kinds of fruit: the fruit of the Spirit,[5] the fruit of righteous living[6] and the fruit of advancing the kingdom.[7] We don't get to pick and choose among the fruit. Every one of us is called to cultivate all three kinds.

Notice the essential role of the fruit of the Spirit—peace, love, joy, patience, kindness, goodness, faithfulness, gentleness, and self-control. If we don't abide in Jesus, the fruit of the Spirit are the first to get spoiled! If we aren't bearing the fruit of the Spirit, whatever work we are doing will have a rotten smell to it. According to Paul, even if we have righteous deeds and kingdom advances to boast of, but have not love, then we "gain nothing."[8] Clearly, the fruit of the Spirit are essential to both life and ministry.

The Key to Our Success

Since abiding in Christ is the only way we can bear fruit, especially the fruit of the Spirit, then abiding is the key to doing ministry. In Jesus own words it is impossible to think of doing things for Jesus without also doing everything we can to abide in Him at the same time. It is not a question of one or the other. We do not get to choose between being active servants or being those who abide in Jesus. We must learn to do both! We have been chosen to "bear fruit" and it is only by abiding that we have any hope of accomplishing our assignment.

If this sounds impossibly hard, it is. We will never learn the way of abiding or of bearing true fruit unless Jesus helps us, but that is exactly what He wants to do. He says that whatever we ask for will be given us. Look what that promise means in this context. Anything we need in order to abide or bear fruit, God will gladly supply! Call on His Name—He will always come to your aid.[9] Return to Him as often as the peace of abiding departs—He will always welcome you back.[10] No one abides in Jesus all of the time. We all lose the peace He gives us, especially in the midst of trials. The great thing is recognizing that you have lost the peace of abiding (once again) and make a quick return!

Seen in this light, seeking to be of service to Jesus, presses us to learn how to abide in Him, and that in turn ushers in all of the inimitable joys of living in His Presence.[11] Truly, His joy enters us as we learn to abide in Him. Once again Jesus demonstrates that His number one concern for us as servants is love: "Abide in My love." From that place of strength, service becomes a joy and the fruit naturally follows.

Jesus overturns our natural bent. We may want success (results) at the work in order to feel confident we have pleased Him and don't mind striving and stressing to get those results. His approach is quite different. He is pleased if we take our confidence from trusting ourselves to His steadfast love. Then He gets to reap the results He wants through us *while we are trusting*.

Two Necessary Steps

How do we allow Jesus to do His ministry through us? Abiding is intimately connected with trusting Jesus for all He allows and obeying Him in what He asks. That is a subject all its own. Nevertheless, there are two steps we need to take at the beginning of any work of ministry. The first step is to consecrate the work to Him; the second step is to consecrate ourselves.

1) Consecrating the Work. We commit our field of service to Him in prayer. Christian work and prayer go hand in hand, because no amount of effort on our part can make up for any failure by us to bring the Lord in as the central player. Always keep in mind that it is His work in us and through us that will win the day. Naturally enough we pray for His blessing, but to ensure that, we commit the work to Him, asking Him to take charge over it and work with us to make sure that His will is done. The Holy Spirit will show what needs to be prayed for and help us with the prayers, but the central thing is truly committing or giving the work to God.[12]

2) Consecrating Ourselves. This needs doing up front in prayer, but it is necessary to keep watch over ourselves all along the way. The key to this is to intentionally place ourselves under His leadership through prayer and the yielding of our wills, just as He showed us was necessary for Him in the Garden: "Not my will, but Thine be done." Whenever we do this in life or in ministry, we have peace.[13] Any loss of peace is a clear call from the Holy Spirit to repent, return to the Lord, be refreshed in His Presence and re-consecrate ourselves to operating under His leadership.[14]

CHAPTER 22

THE HEART OF A SERVANT

There are two sides to cultivating a servant's heart which we see fully revealed in Jesus. They also dove-tail beautifully into fulfilling the two commands He gave us. First, there is the passion to be about the Father's business which keeps us asking "What would You have me do?" This takes us upwards into God's Heart and downwards into the humility that sets Self aside. Second, there is compassion which keeps us looking to the sea of humanity around us, listening for God's call that comes to us through their need.

> **"It shall not be so among you. But whoever would be great among you must be your servant, and whoever would be first among you must be your slave, even as the Son of Man came not to be served but to serve, and to give his life as a ransom for many."** Matthew 20:26-28

The Lowest Place

Where would we be without those opportunistic sons of Zebedee, James and John? Their unabashed desire to one day sit enthroned beside Jesus, provoked the Lord to give us the penetrating look into His kingdom and His calling quoted above.[1] It's not our way, is it? He didn't come to make a name for Himself, or to get anything for Himself, or to be served by us. He came simply and solely to serve us, even to the ultimate end of laying down His life for us. He says that's what He wants us to be like.

With these few words Jesus stands the world on its head. Headship among us is characterized by making sure that others look up to our elevated position, bowing before us in gratitude, respect and obedience. We didn't climb all this way up the mountain for nothing! There's got to be something in it for us. Tragically, the very desire to rise to the top which lies behind so much of our excellence and achieving, comes from the lowest thing about us—our pride.[2] We don't have to rise very high to fall into this snare: Even the slightest elevation can have us looking to see if anyone else noticed our advance or being miffed if they didn't.

Jesus says that in His kingdom the head takes the lowest place.[3] Those who would follow Him must become like Him in being a servant to everyone else. You don't have to be the Pope or the President for this to apply to you. Moral greatness rests upon anyone who learns to be a servant. Those who seek leadership positions—"being first"—must be willing to descend even lower, becoming "slaves." Naturally enough, our own heads aren't going to take this self-debasement lying down! Fortunately, Jesus has given us a new heart, one just like His—the heart of a servant. Look no further: It is already in you, waiting and desiring to emerge.

And I will give you a new heart, and a new spirit I will put within you. And I will remove the heart of stone from your flesh and give you a heart of flesh. Ezekiel 36:26

Growing Your Heart

Our new hearts don't grow all by themselves. Like any tender young plant they require careful cultivation. The basic strategy is to plant your new heart in some field of service, keep watering it with the Word and with worship, and stand ready to pull weeds coming from your fallen nature when they show up. That won't take long. Inevitably, you will discover that there is a battle enjoined between the old ways of our fallen nature which seem so natural to us and the new ways of grace which are sometimes difficult to receive. This has been beautifully captured in song.[4]

Nature and Grace

By John Michael Talbot

Deep within me there lies a true distinction,
Between the things I would and what I really do.
I cannot believe that I am so unusual,
Isn't this the common sorrow within me and you?

Nature will seek only its own advantage.
It considers only how another might be used.
Grace will bring a new humility,
To comfort those afflicted and to help those once abused.

Nature might seek its fair consolation,
But it never offers its help without its price, without reward.
Grace finds reward in another's consolation,
Learning in this paradox the power of our Lord.

Nature will seek to be exalted in authority,
To argue its opinion and to have all the world conform.
Grace humbly comes in a silent assuredness,
Speaking only to conform a man unto His Lord.

Nature might seek its fair consolation,
But it never offers its help without its price, without reward.
Grace finds reward in another's consolation,
Learning in this paradox the power of our Lord.

This heart of a servant within us doesn't seek recognition or reward. Its reward is to be of service. For that it is ever listening for the call, willing to set the demands of life or the desires of Self aside in order to respond to the One who has our ear.[5] Our new hearts live by the law of sacrifice just as Jesus did. [6] By dying to Self we enter into the greater joy of living for God. This new heart works beautifully when everything is going well. Few things give us more pleasure than serving in Jesus' Name. However, it should be evident that this new heart will have a lot of battles to fight, if it is going to triumph over the self-centered ways of our old nature.

If there was a short cut to eliminating Self, so that the new heart could truly flourish, Jesus would have told us. Instead, He warned us that we should be prepared to battle our selfish, self-centered side *daily*.[7] How can we go the distance with so demanding a task?

Going the Distance

The Old Testament gives us a vivid picture of a devoted servant whose love for his master inspired him to go the extra mile. Rather than take his leave when his indentured time was fulfilled, he chose to stay on as a permanent slave. Foreseeing that such a possibility could happen, the Lord made provision for it in His Word.

> **"Now these are the rules that you shall set before them. When you buy a Hebrew slave, he shall serve six years, and in the seventh he shall go out free, for nothing... But if the slave plainly says, 'I love my master, my wife, and my children; I will not go out free,' then his master shall bring him to God, and he shall bring him to the door or the doorpost. And his master shall bore his ear through with an awl, and he shall be his slave forever."** Exodus 21:1-2, 5-6

This may seem incredible to us, even unthinkable. That servant could have walked out a free man, owing nothing. Instead, He freely chose to become a "slave forever." Why? Masters in the ancient world provided food, clothing, bedding and personal security for their servants—the necessities of life. That could have been part of it, but we are simply told that he stayed for love. In a dramatic ceremony the "bond servant" was marked permanently as one whose ear would be forever attuned to his master's voice. He would be listening "at the door," whether he was to go outside on his master's business, or inside to attend to his master's personal requirements. His willingness to suffer and bleed sealed the covenant.

Amazingly, the first apostles referred to themselves in their letters as just such a bond servant. They even introduced themselves as "a bond servant of the Lord Jesus" before they mentioned (oh by the way) that they were also apostles chosen by God.[8] They evidently wanted the world to know that they were sold out to the One who had bought them at the price of His own Blood. Once saved, they could have chosen to live within the wide boundaries of the moral law, but they chose instead to enslave themselves to His will. They only wanted to come and go at His beck and call.

There is a significant difference between mere servants and bond servants. Good servants may still cherish and prefer their free time apart from doing their master's bidding. Bond servants seek only time at their master's side. Since our Master lives inside of us, this is surely the most searching form of slavery imaginable, with every thought, word and action coming under the scrutiny of our Lord's all pervasive presence. And yet, wonder of wonder, in His service we find our perfect freedom! God and Jesus only desire for us that which we ourselves would gladly choose if we had Their wisdom and foresight. Those who go deepest into loving service He raises highest into spiritual friendship.[9] The devoted servant and the kind-hearted Master are intimately intertwined—serving one another in love.

Two Motivations

We have not one, but two vast reservoirs of motivation for active service, whose ultimate source is in the heart of our God. It is, therefore, technically impossible to burn out or dry up if—and that is a really big *if*—you learn how to stay well-connected to Jesus. Seen in the right light, this provides extra incentive for staying active in ministry because serving others is one of those things that press us deeper into Christ, if we let it.[10]

1) **Passion.** Our first and most powerful source of motivation grows out of God's love for us and ours for Him.[11] This can be easily renewed whenever we return and rest our hearts in Him.[12] This is the secret of the bond servant. By always seeking to be at His side listening for our next assignment, there is a built-in reminder for staying refreshed by His Presence.[13] Learning to walk step-by-step under the Lord's leadership ensures that we will spend our days seeking Him, because like Moses, we won't desire to go anywhere without His Presence leading us.[14] You don't have to be especially good at this, just doggedly determined.[15]

2) **Compassion.** Our second source of motivation mirrors the Second Commandment that the Lord gave us: to love one another

as we love ourselves. Provided that we have learned to accept and love ourselves, our hearts will naturally want to share with others the peace, joy and freedom that keep flooding into us. Because our passion for Jesus is filling our cup, we don't need to use people or get anything from them. We are free to serve them under His leadership, expecting nothing in return. It is enough to know that He knows. This is our baseline, but we can go deeper. We can want to see what He sees and feel what He feels when He looks into the lives around us. In this way our passion for Him, leads us into greater compassion for others.

Not only do we have these two passionate purposes to keep ourselves fired up for active service, we also have two monumental tasks: to take the liberating gospel out to the lost world and to carry loving compassion into the hurting world. That should keep us busy! But don't let busyness keep you from the most important part of it all: Loving Jesus and loving the ones He loves. Growing a heart of love is our underlying purpose in ministry and our source of lasting joy. Gaining the heart of a servant will carry us a long way towards home.

CHAPTER 23

THE CARE OF SOULS

The people we pass every day on the streets will outlast the Grand Canyon and are of infinitely more worth than any governmental structure. How are we to handle them, especially when they come to us for ministry? Some are obviously stamped "Fragile, Handle with Care." Others have their secret life hidden further from sight. We can easily be like bulls in a china shop, if we don't take care with souls.

"So whatever you wish that others would do to you, do also to them, for this is the Law and the Prophets."
Matthew 7:12

Let "the Rule" Rule

Try as we might we will never be able to improve on this saying of the Lord. His Golden Rule could easily guide all of our efforts to minister to others. Just put yourself in their place and imagine how you would like to be treated. Imagine what you would be feeling; how you might be acting out; how you would be hoping that someone out there could sympathize and understand. Imagine how much an undeserved gesture of kindness or gentleness would mean to you. Would you want tender comfort? Or the truth kindly, but honestly spoken? Would you be grateful for anyone who could sense your pain? Or lift your spirits?

Without a doubt the Golden Rule should rule! But being the kind of folks that we are, we need clarification points to pin to our conscience so that we will recognize the moment when it is upon us. We are so secretly good at flipping the rule: expecting others to treat us as we want them to! Jesus never gave us permission to go at life that way. I have to treat them as I would want to be treated, but they are free to treat me however they like—I still have to treat them by the Rule.[1] So, let's resolve right at the beginning that we are going to live by the Lord's Rule even if others don't! Now for some points of further clarification.

Caring for Souls

Caring for souls primarily means taking care of their hearts.[2] You can feed a hungry homeless person a great meal, but if you treat them with disrespect, they will walk out emptier than when they came in. Similarly, you can minister to a hurting believer through prayers that have you both in tears, but if you tell others their secret, they will wish they never knew you. Here's a truth you can take to the bank: If the person needing ministry knew how to take care of their own heart, they wouldn't need you to minister to them. That's why we have to take such care with them. Their heart is what the Lord is after. Their heart is where He wants to dwell. Their heart is the key to all the other issues in their life.

> **Keep your heart with all diligence, for out of it spring the issues of life.** Proverbs 4:23 NKJV

To care for others at the level of taking care of their hearts, means that we will have to attend to the needs of our own heart in the process. Jesus said that we should love others as we love ourselves.[3] This carries a subtle inference that the proper love of self is necessary for the proper love of others: We will love them as (to the extent that) we love ourselves. If accepting, forgiving and loving yourself as God loves you is hard for you, don't you imagine that hardness against yourself will get in the way of accepting, forgiving and loving others? Indeed it does! There is real help for this: Please see "Love Thyself!" at our website for healing, healingstreamsusa.org.

In the meantime focus on this: The way that Jesus loves us is what we want to pass on to others. His love is what it's all about. This means that we will have to get very good (as we go along) at receiving His mercy and love, so that we will keep having a good supply of it to share with others.

I. Giving Comfort

One of the easiest things to do for others and certainly one of the most meaningful is to give comfort. As long as you keep in mind that giving comfort is not fixing them or fixing their situation, you will do well and you will be able to do it without getting stressed up. The problem comes when we just can't bear to see them suffering either so much or for so long. That's when we may succumb to the temptation to rescue them, putting the too-heavy burden of their life on our frail shoulders. Always remember that there is only One Person who is fully qualified to do that. Look to see the part you can do (with His grace helping you) and *leave the really heavy lifting to Jesus.*

Job's friends are a classic example of people who started out giving comfort, but later gave in to the temptation to fix the problem which they mistakenly took to be Job himself. As long as they sat with him in silence sharing his pain, they did well. Moreover, there was nothing back-breaking about the assignment. It comes naturally to us to "weep with those who weep."[4] They blew it, however, when they lost patience both with Job (who was becoming a pill) and with the Lord (who wasn't acting fast enough to resolve things). If all you can think to do is commiserate with and befriend the hurting person that is all you need to do. Beyond this, it often helps to remember how the Lord brought genuine comfort to you in a similar situation and see if that shows you some further part you can play.

> **Blessed be the God and Father of our Lord Jesus Christ, the Father of mercies and God of all comfort, who comforts us in all our affliction, so that we may be able to comfort those who are in any affliction, with the comfort with which we ourselves are comforted by God.**
> 2 Corinthians 1:3-4

II. Guarding Confidence

It is safe to say that no one will have any confidence in us if we cannot keep a confidence that they share with us. Don't think just in terms of secrets that may be shared in confessional moments. These certainly must be guarded with the utmost concern for their privacy.

However, there are many things of an intimate nature that may come to our attention when ministering to others: the way they look or how they behave; the way their house looks; their family relationships or financial situation. Whatever comfort the Lord may give them through us will be stripped away if we don't guard these privileged glimpses into their lives.

People who are suffering pain or lack are already humbled and vulnerable if they have sought others out for help. In a very real sense they are standing before us with their naked need exposed. Nakedness in scripture represents that which would give us shame if openly displayed. Think of Adam and Eve instinctively reaching for those fig leaves. Paul wrote that just as we treat our "unpresentable parts" with greater modesty, so in the Body of Christ we are meant to clothe the weaker members with greater honor, taking care to guard their dignity.[5] Furthermore, it seems that the Lord took a dim view of Noah's son who exposed his father's "nakedness"—even though Noah had behaved in a disreputable way.[6] When in doubt, keep quiet about it.

> **Never repeat what you are told and you will come to no harm; whether to friend or foe, do not talk about it, unless it would be sinful not to, do not reveal it; you would be heard out, then mistrusted, and in due course you would be hated. Have you heard something? Let it die with you. Courage! It will not burst you!**
> Ecclesiasticus 19:7-10 TJB (the Apocrypha)

III. Genuine Courtesy

The rules of etiquette and the traditional courtesies originated as ways for showing respect to others.[7] They still work. Key among these is the willingness to take the time to look people in the eyes, to listen carefully to what they are saying and to share empathetically with their plight. This goes a long ways towards helping them. Not only does it enable you to access their situation more accurately (so that you can give better care), but it immediately gives them the comfort of being treated with dignity, as someone who is worth your time. The care of souls and an assembly line approach to solving human problems are completely incompatible! If you put people on the clock they always know it, and feel diminished. It is a breach of common courtesy.

No one exhibited the divine grace that lies within genuine courtesy better than St. Francis of Assisi. Be sure to read about him when you have time and if you don't have time, make time.[8] He was called "the mirror of perfection" in his day—the medieval world marveled at the ways Jesus shined out through his every word or deed. He made it a point of personal honor never to meet anyone who was poorer than himself. This kept his brother monks busy finding better things for him to wear because he was forever exchanging his garments with every beggar he met. Let that image penetrate you: The heart of courtesy is to treat other souls as if they matter more to you than your own immediate comfort.

> So if there is any encouragement in Christ, any comfort from love, any participation in the Spirit, any affection and sympathy, complete my joy by being of the same mind, having the same love, being in full accord and of one mind. Do nothing from rivalry or conceit, but in humility count others more significant than yourselves. Let each of you look not only to his own interests, but also to the interests of others. Philippians 2:1-4

Holy Spirit

CHAPTER 24

THE ART OF LISTENING

Hearing what people say is one thing. Really listening is something else entirely. What turns listening into an art form is learning how to juggle listening to others and listening for the Lord at the same time. Listen well enough to others and you will more easily hear from the Lord. These simple rules and visual images will help put you on track, but only practice makes perfect.

And he said, "He who has ears to hear, let him hear." Mark 4:9

A Lost Art

Sometime in the last century we lost the art of letter writing. Once widespread and flourishing, writing long, thoughtful letters by hand kept people intimately in touch over great distances, but the telephone and air travel supplanted it. Something similar seems to be happening to story tellers and good listeners. Where are the raconteurs who could hold you spell bound with a simple tale lovingly told? Where are the caring souls who set their lives aside to really give a good listen to yours? It seems as if both are being crowded out by the pressured pace of modern life, for both of these art forms require a gracious supply of time in which to thrive.

This cultural deficit actually makes our task as Christian ministers much easier. So many people are weighted down or stressed up with the burdens they are carrying. Often their attempts to find a caring soul have been brushed off by people too busy to give them the time of day. Others they encountered were so filled with their own cares they didn't dare open themselves to feeling the weight of another's concern. And then there were false friends who heard them out, but failed to keep the confidence. In such a cultural climate finding a good listener is a rare treasure indeed! Yet, listening is the easiest point of access for those who desire to enter into the care of souls which is the essence of Christian ministry.

The beautiful thing about becoming a good listener is a) that you can start right away and b) you can easily do a lot of good and very little harm.[1] The deeper you go into Christian ministry the more training you will need and the more danger there will be of inadvertently causing damage. If you want to counsel people, or exercise a gift of prophecy, or minister inner healing and deliverance, you'll have to strap yourself in for the long haul. Seeking to help people at the level of their deepest need requires training and teamwork.[2] But if you want to relieve people by listening well, all you need is one good ear. If you have two, so much the better!

Ears to Hear Him

Listening is also important because our life with God is predicated upon listening carefully. In fact our ability to listen to others will increase dramatically as we learn how to give ear to the Lord. He speaks His word to us in a variety of ways. We listen for what He may be saying to us through scripture, through the words of others, through books, through conscience and through the way the Spirit guides our circumstances. That's a lot of listening! But that is not all.

There is an art to listening to the Lord. If you stay busy, you hear very little. The more you slow down, the more you notice that He just might be trying to get your attention about something. Then, if you really settle down and get quiet, you just might (finally) be in the right position to hear what He is saying. Imagine a darkened, windswept, rain-splattered pond. If an acorn were to drop on the surface you'd hardly notice. However, let that same pond be utterly still on a sunny day and anything dropped on the surface will be immediately heard and its effects seen across the whole expanse of quiet water. Learn to be that quiet pond on the inside and you will hear so much better from the Lord. How will we ever understand our lives or our world, if we don't pause to really hear Him when He speaks?

And he called the people to him and said to them, "Hear and understand." Matthew 15:10

All of this training at listening to the Lord comes in handy when listening to people. With them also it is not just a simple matter of recognizing and understanding words. The way they speak, their choice of words, their inflections, pauses and points of emphasis all give insight into their inner conversation—the thoughts of their heart. Body language and facial expressions also send a message, sometimes more loudly than anything they may actually be saying. If a person looks really down and discouraged and you hear it in their voice, but they tell you "all's well," what are you going to listen to as truth?

Just as we need to be quiet to hear from the Lord, so too we need to be quiet to listen well to others. Being unquiet on the inside always gets in the way of good listening. Haven't we all seen people at parties who can't wait for the other person to finish speaking, so they can jump in? Many people, when introduced to someone new, are so anxious what to say that they don't hear and remember the person's name. Or, perhaps something you heard triggered a very distracting thought. By the time you came to the end of it, you looked up and realized the other person was still speaking to you! These are just a few examples to show the need for emptying out as soon as you turn your attention to someone who wants to open up to you.

Stop, Look and Listen

We have to be ready to give our complete attention at a moment's notice. Years ago we had railroad signs in this country which said, "Railroad Crossing: Stop, Look and Listen." If you don't want to wreck the other person's train of thought, let this bygone phrase remind you of the danger of not coming to a full stop! Then, let the whole phrase provide a framework for excellent listening.

I. Stop!

As soon as you see that someone wants to open up to you, or has a legitimate need to talk, stop what you're doing. This should be obvious, but the devil is in the details. If you look at your watch, or fidget, or show the slightest sign of irritation or impatience, you may lose your moment with them. Come to a full stop and *stay* stopped. Set the stuff in you aside. Don't start thinking of other things you could be doing, unless of course, you should be doing them. In that case it is better to listen well to the first few sentences, explain that you have to go, but would really like to hear more later. Honesty like this will save you from resentment and them from embarrassment.

Inconvenience, on the other hand, can conceal the call of the Lord. Moses famously turned aside upon seeing the burning bush — it wasn't his plan.[3] Had he not noticed and stopped, he could easily have missed out on joining the Lord in a very heroic part of the Rescue. If you don't know it yet, you may as well brace yourself for finding it out soon: The Lord takes a rather cavalier attitude towards our agendas.[4] He prefers His plans to ours! Imagine. This means that your burning bush moments with others may come at seemingly inopportune times. Take time to tune in to the Lord. Lift the interruption immediately up to Him. If you can't honorably set it aside, set your agenda aside instead. He'll help you with that later.

II. Look!

Above all, look them in the eyes. Look with your heart of love and acceptance that Jesus gives you.[5] Look to see how important this moment is to them. Just don't overwhelm them by too intense a gaze — people in need often feel insecure and wilt if you look into them too deeply or too long. Then, as you have opportunity, take in the whole aspect of the person to see what that might tell you as you begin listening to them. Are they in a pain or a panic? Do they seem distressed and disheveled? Do they look like they need an immediate response from you to calm them down? How badly do they seem to be in need? Will someone else have to be called in, or does this seem like something you (with the Lord's help) can handle?

While you're looking, look around. Is this a good place for the person to open up? Will it afford them enough privacy? Do they seem on the brink of tears? In that case is there a quieter corner or more convenient place for the conversation? If you are feeling self-conscious or awkward about being approached, try not to let it show. Above all, never worry how the situation will look to others. Deal with those feelings immediately by looking up to the Lord and seeing or sensing if you have a green light from Him to go forward in this location. That's all that matters. Very likely you will get the go ahead, since the burning bush moment is already a sign of His Providence in choosing the time and place. If not, suggest a better location and move there.

III. Listen!

James tells us to be quick to listen, slow to speak.[6] That's our guide. Affirm their feelings, not necessarily their opinions. Wait patiently for your time to speak—don't interrupt. Be willing to count your own words as small things compared to what the Lord will be speaking to them, simply by you listening well. The image here is of a full pitcher of water. They are filled to the brim with all kinds of thoughts and feelings. If they don't tell someone they will overflow!

Your job is to let them pour what's inside them out upon your listening ears. It hardly matters where they begin. Their heart will secretly direct their conversation to the points that really matter. That's where you want to focus your innermost attention: on whatever it is that their heart is seeking to express. Don't strain. Just listen to them and to the Lord. If some insight needs to come to you, it will. Once that comes out into the open, your own heart will help you give the right response when it's your turn to speak. If you can find nothing significant to share, don't reproach yourself. Keep listening! Turning on the lights for you and your friend is the Lord's job. We are wisest when we wait on Him to do just that.

In the meantime, remember that we weep with those who weep and laugh with those who laugh. Both are healing.[7] Just go with the flow at first, responding to them as Jesus does with you. Set aside any judgments that may arise against their situation or their behavior. Ask questions if need be to keep the flow going: "What hurts? How did that make you feel?" Be a spiritual sponge! Absorb what they are sharing, taking it to your own heart and holding it up to the Lord in prayer. Be directive or assertive only if they seem to be straying off focus or dodging something. Good listening creates a bond of trust. You have to earn the right to speak.

As they empty out, this give you the opportunity to pour in some encouragement or the wisdom gained from a similar experience.[8] Just don't be in a hurry to do that. The quarry is dove like. If you don't quietly wait for your moment, you may startle them into taking flight. The primary comfort is not your words, but your love. That is shown incredibly well by listening well. It is rightly said that a burden shared is half lifted — and you don't even have to do any of the lifting. The Lord will lift their spirit through the principle of fellowship.

Hospitality to Strangers

Good listening is a way of showing "hospitality to strangers."[9] Perhaps you already know them to some degree. Nevertheless, their problems reveal an inner depth and strangeness — the fundamental *estrangement* from God and others that all of us suffer from in one way or another. By listening well you are welcoming them into your presence and treating their conversation with the respect a guest of your house deserves. God will use your caring and listening heart to bring much comfort and restoration, even if you have no inspired insight to give. Just by talking out loud people are helped, even to the point of discovering the answer for themselves. Just know your limits. Avoid sharing about unhealed, wounded areas in your life and getting in too deep into theirs. Follow these simple guidelines and you will not only do others a great deal of good, you will be making friends for eternity as you go along.

GODSPEED

Every journey is meant to take us somewhere or what's the point of going? Where will you be heading with yours? There are many possible outcomes to the path of life set before you, but there are only two destinations which just happen to match up with the Lord's two great commands. One direction will take you into the Heart of God. The other will take you into finding your place in the Rescue. If all goes well these two directions will converge in an extended season of fruitful harvest and joyful intimacy. Before you get there, however, there will be many a challenge along the way. No doubt that's why Jesus has given us His Holy Spirit to be our Comforter, Guide and Travelling Companion. May you discover that He is everything set forth in this little book—and more!

Godspeed may sound funny to our ears, but the idea behind it was eminently sensible. It expressed a devout wish for the Lord to prosper a friend or loved one on their journey. I pray that He will prosper yours.

Appendix

To our God and Father be glory forever and ever. Amen.
The grace of the Lord Jesus Christ be with your spirit.
Philippians 4:20, 23

ENDNOTES

Chapter 1: Hosting a Mystery

[1] Because He is the Spirit of the Father and sent by both Father and Son, it is entirely appropriate to use the male pronoun when speaking of Him. Jesus did. As one example see John 14:26-27: *But the Helper, the Holy Spirit... he will teach you all things.*

[2] Daniel 7:9: *As I looked... the Ancient of days took his seat; his clothing was white as snow, and the hair of his head like pure wool;* Revelation 4:2-3: *A throne stood in heaven, with one seated on the throne. And he who sat there had the appearance of jasper and carnelian...*

Chapter 2: Holy Spirit Our Helper

[1] Ephesians 1:13-14: *Sealed with the promised Holy Spirit ...*

[2] From the very beginning, God has been "doing" what He does by the powerful working of the Holy Spirit: Genesis 1:1-2: *In the beginning... the Spirit of God...*

[3] Psalms 104:30: *You send forth Your Spirit and give them breath...*

[4] Holy Spirit our Helper will be with us eternally: John 14:16-17: *Another Helper, to be with you forever...*

[5] As you can see by this verse the "new and living way" is through faith in what Jesus has done for us, but that we are meant to strive for "the full assurance of faith"—a life characterized by the peace-confidence that comes through total surrender: Hebrews 10:22: *By the new and living way... let us draw near with a true heart in full assurance of faith.*

[6] Matthew 18:3 AMP: *Repent (change, turn about) and become like little children [trusting, lowly, loving, forgiving]...*

[7] Here is just one example of how the Spirit works through us: Matthew 10:19-20: *For it is not you who speak, but the Spirit of your Father speaking through you.*

[8] Ephesians 3:20-21: *Far more abundantly than all that we ask or think...*

[9] Galatians 2:20: *It is no longer I who live, but Christ who lives in me...*

[10] Ezekiel 36:26: *And I will give you a new heart, and a new spirit...*

[11] God makes an unconditional promise that all who call on Him will be saved (think helped, rescued, delivered) in one situation after another: Romans 10:13.

[12] It takes putting "the flesh" to death (fear, anger, worry, wrong desire, etc.), by choosing to trust Jesus and do what He says. Then the fruit of the Spirit supernaturally appears: Galatians 5:22-24: *The fruit of the Spirit... have crucified the flesh with its passions and desires.*

[13] John 7:37-39: *Out of his heart will flow rivers of living water...*

[14] Isaiah 66:12: *Behold, I will extend peace to her like a river...*

[15] John 6:28-29: *This is the work of God, that you believe in him...*

[16] John 15:26: *The Helper... will bear witness about me.*

[17] Throughout this book I will be capitalizing "Self" to indicate the fallen condition of living unsurrendered to Christ under the rule of our own self-will. This is the supreme "work of the flesh" which places our lives at enmity with God and His will for us. When "self" simply means ourselves as the person God created and loves, I have left it in lower

case. Galatians 5:18-19: *But if you are led by the Spirit, you are not under the law. Now the works of the flesh are evident.*

[18] John 14:26 *The Holy Spirit... bring to your remembrance all that I have said to you.*

[19] We need that especially, because thinking there won't be negative consequences is what makes doing the wrong thing seems so appealing.

[20] After the disaster of his sin with Bathsheba, King David saw the need for the Holy Spirit's help in sustaining him with a spirit willing to do what God desired: Psalms 51:12 WEB: *Restore to me the joy of your salvation. Uphold me with a willing spirit.*

Chapter 3: New Life in the Spirit

[1] The "gold standard" for evidence of having received saving faith is given by Paul in Romans and these disciples would have easily passed on both counts: Romans 10:9-10: *If you confess with your mouth that Jesus is Lord and believe in your heart...*

[2] In his on-the-scene explanation of the events of Pentecost Peter specifically identified the promise of the Father in Joel as being the one which Jesus had called them to seek: Acts 2:14-17: *This is what was uttered through the prophet Joel...*

Chapter 4: Holy Spirit, Jesus and You

[1] Hebrews 2:14-18: *He had to be made like his brothers in every respect...*

[2] Our confidence in God's loving plans for us is what gives the Lord pleasure; He can take "no pleasure" when we "draw back" since such fearfulness is never in our best interest: Hebrews 10:37-39: *If he shrinks back, my soul has no pleasure in him...*

[3] Matthew 3:13-15: *John would have prevented him...*

[4] John 5:19: *The Son can do nothing of his own accord...*

[5] Luke 11:20: *It is by the finger of God [the Holy Spirit] that I cast out demons...*

[6] John 14:12: *Whoever believes in me will also do the works that I do...*

[7] Psalms 45:7: *God has anointed you with the oil of gladness...*

Chapter 5: The Indwelling Presence

[1] Ephesians 1:13-14: *Holy Spirit, who is the guarantee of our inheritance...*

[2] John 3:6-7 AMP: *Being born of the Spirit (the Holy Spirit), or being born from above.*

[3] John 16:12-14: *He will take what is mine and declare it to you.*

[4] John 16:7: *It is to your advantage that I go away...*

[5] This evocative phrase comes to us from the list of faith's heroes in the 11th Chapter of Hebrews. Jesus has surely won this for us: Hebrews 11:35 NKJV: *Others were tortured, not accepting deliverance, that they might obtain a better resurrection.*

[6] John 20:27-29 AMP: *Do not be faithless...but [stop your unbelief and] believe!*

[7] Jesus apparently thought it necessary that He ascend so that the Holy Spirit could take His place as an indwelling presence: John 14:16: *For he dwells with you and will be in you.*

[8] In this passage Paul speaks of our sanctification in the past tense as something already accomplished: 1 Corinthians 6:11: *But you were washed, you were sanctified...*

[9] Here Paul speaks of sanctification as a present tense process of being shown truth (by the Holy Spirit) and then believing the truth (also with the Spirit's help): 2 Thessalonians 2:13 AMP: *Through the sanctifying work of the [Holy] Spirit…*

[10] John 16:13: *When the Spirit of truth comes, he will guide you into all the truth.*

[11] John 16:8-11: *Convict the world concerning sin and righteousness and judgment.*

[12] Galatians 2:20 AMP: *It is no longer I who live, but Christ (the Messiah) lives in me.*

[13] Romans 8:21 KJV: *The glorious liberty of the children of God.*

[14] Galatians 5:22: *But the fruit of the Spirit is love, joy, peace, patience…*

[15] John 7:37-39: *Out of his heart will flow rivers of living water.*

Chapter 6: True Spiritual Health

[1] Beware of self will—it is the core sin of pride that took Lucifer down: Isaiah 14:12-15: *How you are fallen from heaven, O Day Star [Lucifer], son of Dawn! How you are cut down to the ground, you who laid the nations low! You said in your heart, 'I will ascend to heaven; above the stars of God I will set my throne on high…' But you are brought down to Sheol...*

[2] 2 Corinthians 4:3-6: *The god of this world has blinded the minds of the unbelievers, to keep them from seeing the light of the gospel of the glory of Christ.*

[3] 2 Corinthians 4:6: *For God… has shone in our hearts to give the light of the knowledge of the glory of God in the face of Jesus Christ.*

[4] 2 Corinthians 3:16-18: *With unveiled face, beholding the glory of the Lord, are being transformed into the same image from one degree of glory to another.*

[5] 2 Corinthians 5:14-15: *He died for all, that those who live might no longer live for themselves but for him who for their sake died and was raised.*

[6] Psalms 51:12 NASB: *Sustain me with a willing spirit.*

[7] See Isaiah 6:1-8 for the prophet's experience during a throne room visit.

[8] 2 Corinthians 10:4-5: *For the weapons of our warfare… have divine power to destroy strongholds. We… take every thought captive to obey Christ.*

Chapter 7: Walking in the Spirit

[1] Galatians 5:25: *If we live by the Spirit, let us also walk by the Spirit.*

[2] Psalm 138:2 AMP: *You have magnified Your word above all Your name!*

[3] Ephesians 5:25: *As Christ loved the church and gave himself up for her.*

[4] Ephesians 1:13: *Sealed with the promised Holy Spirit.*

[5] John 20:22: *He breathed on them and said to them, "Receive the Holy Spirit."*

[6] Ephesians 2:8: *For by grace you have been saved through faith…*

[7] Isaiah 46:3-4: *Who have been borne by me from before your birth.*

[8] Matthew 18:2-4: *Like this child is the greatest in the kingdom of heaven.*

[9] Isaiah 11:6: *A little child shall lead them.* See also Mark 10:15; Luke 18:17.

[10] Isaiah 42:5: *Who gives breath to the people on it and spirit to those who walk in it.*

[11] John 14:16-18: *He dwells with you and will be in you.*

[12] John 1:4, 9: *In him was life, and the life was the light of men…*

[13] Saint Augustine of Hippo (354-430 AD), Seventh Homily on 1st John.

[14] Galatians 2:20: *It is no longer I who live, but Christ who lives in me.*

[15] Proverbs 3:5-6 KJV: *In all thy ways acknowledge him, and he shall direct thy paths.*

16 Hannah Whitall Smith, *The Christian's Secret of a Happy Life* (New York, NY: Ballantine Books, 1986), p. 81.

17 Ezekiel 47:1-5 WEB: *Waters to swim in, a river that could not be passed through.*

Chapter 8: Guided by the Spirit

1 Ephesians 5:15-18: *Walk, not as unwise, but as wise… understand what the will of the Lord is.*

2 1 Kings 22:7-8 especially verse 8: *I hate him, for he never prophesies good concerning me…*

3 Hannah Whitall Smith, *The Christian's Secret of a Happy Life* (New York, NY: Ballantine Books, 1986), p. 79.

4 Ibid., p 72. The "voices" of guidance are expanded from the chapter "Difficulties Concerning Guidance." Consensus of wise counsel has been added to the four "voices" listed in *The Christian's Secret* op. cit.

5 See Psalm 119—all of it.

6 It was Jesus' prayer for us: John 17:17: *Sanctify them in the truth; your word is truth.*

7 The first commandment is our foremost assignment and abiding purpose. Mark 12:30: *And you shall love the Lord your God with all your heart…*

8 Psalms 119:105: *Your word is a lamp to my feet and a light to my path.*

9 Proverbs 4:5-7 WEB: *Get wisdom. Get understanding.*

10 Romans 12:2: *Be transformed by the renewal of your mind.* Also 2 Thessalonians 2:13.

11 Proverbs 3:5-6: *Trust in the Lord… and do not lean on your own understanding.*

12 James 1:5-6: *If any of you lacks wisdom, let him ask God, who gives generously…*

13 Hebrews 5:14: *Those who have their powers of discernment trained by constant practice.*

14 Isaiah 58:11: *And the Lord will guide you continually.*

15 Micah 6:8: *Do justice, and to love kindness, and to walk humbly with your God.*

16 James 4:6: *God opposes the proud, but gives grace to the humble.*

17 Matthew 11:19: *Yet wisdom is justified by her deeds.*

18 Psalm 131:1-3: *But I have calmed and quieted my soul, like a weaned child…*

19 1 Kings 19:12: *And after the fire the sound of a low whisper…*

20 Jeremiah 17:9: *The heart is deceitful above all things… who can understand it?*

21 Smith, 76.

22 Proverbs 15:22: *Without counsel plans fail, but with many advisers they succeed.*

23 Proverbs 13:14: *The teaching of the wise is a fountain of life…*

24 Jeremiah 31:34: *No longer shall each one teach his neighbor and each his brother, saying, 'Know the Lord,' for they shall all know me, from the least of them to the greatest.*

25 Revelation 3:7-8: *I have set before you an open door, which no one is able to shut.*

26 John 14:6: *Jesus said to him, "I am the way, and the truth, and the life."*

27 John 10:27: *My sheep hear my voice, and I know them, and they follow me.*

Chapter 9: Spiritual Warfare

1 "Trust and Obey" is the title of a well-loved hymn written by John H. Sammis (1846-1919) which perfectly sums up all that is required for us to live with confidence and joy: *"Trust and obey, trust and obey, there's no other way, to be happy in Jesus, but to trust and obey."*

2 Just imagine Jesus saying to you each morning: "Here is the main thing I want you to be doing today." Would you do it? Now, realize that this is *exactly* what He is saying to all of

us: Matthew 22:37-38: *And he said to him, "You shall love the Lord your God with all your heart and with all your soul and with all your mind. This is the great and first commandment."*

[3] No one expressed it better (or lived it more passionately) than Paul: Galatians 2:20: *I have been crucified with Christ. It is no longer I who live, but Christ who lives in me. And the life I now live in the flesh I live by faith in the Son of God, who loved me and gave himself for me.*

[4] Colossians 3:15: *And let the peace of Christ rule in your hearts.*

[5] Proverbs 4:23: *Keep your heart with all vigilance, for from it flow the springs of life.*

[6] Isaiah 64:8: *But now, O Lord, you are our Father; we are the clay, and you are our potter; we are all the work of your hand;* Romans 9:20-21: *Will what is molded say to its molder, "Why have you made me like this?" Has the potter no right over the clay?*

[7] Matthew 11:27: *No one knows the Son except the Father, and no one knows the Father except the Son and anyone to whom the Son chooses to reveal him.*

[8] 2 Corinthians 4:6: *For God... has shone in our hearts to give the light of the knowledge of the glory of God in the face of Jesus Christ.*

[9] 1 Peter 5:6: *Humble yourselves, therefore, under the mighty hand of God so that at the proper time he may exalt you.*

[10] Galatians 5:22: *But the fruit of the Spirit is love, joy, peace, patience, kindness, goodness, faithfulness, gentleness, self-control... those who belong to Christ Jesus have crucified the flesh with its passions and desires.*

[11] Temptation aims to "draw" our focus away from Jesus to something else: James 1:14 WEB: *But each one is tempted, when he is drawn away by his own lust, and enticed.*

[12] Jack Deere, seminar notes, MorningStar Ministry, Charlotte, NC. September 2005.

[13] Nehemiah 4:17-18: *Those who carried burdens were loaded in such a way that each labored on the work with one hand and held his weapon with the other. And each of the builders had his sword strapped at his side while he built;* Isaiah 60:18: *You shall call your walls Salvation, and your gates Praise.*

Chapter 10: The Baptism of Power

[1] Acts 1:5: *John baptized with water, but you will be baptized with the Holy Spirit...*

[2] Or "a regular person" as I used to be until I got seminary trained. Sadly, professional theological training didn't help with moving in the supernatural. It actually helped "kill" it off me for a while. Seminary can devour the "simple faith" needed for God to work.

[3] In Luke 10:17-20 we see the disciples' delight in the supernatural power that Jesus had entrusted them with. It is so great that Jesus sought to refocus their attention away from their recent experience, back to their eternal position: *Do not rejoice in this, that the spirits are subject to you, but rejoice that your names are written in heaven;* In Luke 9:1-6 we are simply told that the twelve were "healing everywhere": *And they departed and went through the villages, preaching the gospel and healing everywhere.*

[4] Luke 24:48-49: *Stay in the city until you are clothed with power from on high.*

[5] The birth of the modern Pentecostal movement took place in a stable at Azusa Street in Los Angeles, California during a revival that began in 1906 and went around the world.

[6] The "starter kit" includes, but is not limited to: 1) Knowing who Jesus is, 2) Experiencing the forgiveness of our sins, 3) Receiving the hope of heaven, 4) Having the Holy Spirit within us, and 5) Believing that the Bible is God's Word.

[7] 1 Corinthians 12:10: *To another the ability to distinguish between spirits.*

8 This is merely one of many examples of the way the gospel spread. For more simply enter "signs and wonders" into a search program: Acts 14:3: *The Lord, who bore witness to the word of his grace, granting signs and wonders to be done by their hands.*

Chapter 11: Praying in Tongues

1 Jesus first gave the command to wait for this empowerment on the evening of His resurrection (50 days earlier): Luke 24:49: *Stay in the city until you are clothed with power from on high*; Later, on the day of His Ascension (10 days earlier), He repeated the command: Acts 1:4-8: *You will receive power when the Holy Spirit has come upon you.*
2 The group included Mary, mother of Jesus, and other women who had been following Jesus: Acts 1:14: *Together with the women and Mary the mother of Jesus, and his brothers.*
3 Paul's directions in 1 Corinthians 14 make it clear that the preferred Early Church practice was to have someone give an interpretation for publically uttered tongues, if those tongues were a part of a public worship service in which unbelievers might be present. That's not the case here—the unbelievers were outside and only came around when they heard the commotion. What they overheard were private prayer tongues in earthly languages (their own), a phenomenon well-attested to in Pentecostal and Charismatic circles in our day. The "gift of tongues" for public utterance is a manifestation of the Spirit conveying a prophetic message that needs interpretation. It is "apportioned" by the Holy Spirit in a specific situation, unlike the private prayer language which (once given) is under the individual's ability to begin and end. See the "Nine Gifts of Power."
4 Luke 5:36-38: *But new wine must be put into fresh wineskins.*
5 With the Protestant Reformation came the understanding and the phrase that we are saved by "grace alone, through faith alone, in Christ alone."
6 1 Corinthians 12:7-11: *To each is given the manifestation of the Spirit for the common good. To one is given through the Spirit the utterance of wisdom... the utterance of knowledge... faith... gifts of healing... the working of miracles... prophecy... the ability to distinguish between spirits... various kinds of tongues... the interpretation of tongues. All these are empowered by one and the same Spirit, who apportions to each one individually as he wills.*

Chapter 12: The Etiquette of Intimacy

1 Galatians 5:25 KJV: *If we live in the Spirit, let us also walk in the Spirit.*
2 John 17:21: *That they may all be one, just as you, Father, are in me, and I in you, that they also may be in us.*
3 John 15:16: *So that whatever you ask the Father in my name, he may give it to you*; John 14:13: *Whatever you ask in my name, this I will do, that the Father may be glorified in the Son.*
4 John 15:26: *But when the Helper comes... he will bear witness about me.*
5 This kind of craven fear is what characterizes the demons: James 2:19: *You believe that God is one; you do well. Even the demons believe—and shudder!* On the other hand, knowing God's love is the antidote to all ungodly fear: 1 John 4:18: *There is no fear in love, but perfect love casts out fear. For fear has to do with punishment, and whoever fears has not been perfected in love.*
6 Genesis 3:10 WEB: *The man said, "I heard your voice in the garden, and I was afraid, because I was naked; and I hid myself."*

⁷⁷ There is no jealousy in the Godhead, only a fervent desire to honor One Another: Ephesians 1:10 AMP: *[He planned] for the maturity of the times and the climax of the ages to unify all things and head them up and consummate them in Christ, [both] things in heaven and things on the earth.*

⁸ John 14:17: *Even the Spirit of truth... You know him, for he dwells with you and will be in you.*

⁹ The Holy Spirit is the "umpire" who watches over the peace of Christ: Colossians 3:15 AMP: *And let the peace (soul harmony which comes) from Christ rule (act as umpire continually) in your hearts [deciding and settling with finality all questions that arise in your minds, in that peaceful state] to which as [members of Christ's] one body you were also called [to live]. And be thankful (appreciative), [giving praise to God always].*

¹⁰ John 1:32: *And John bore witness: "I saw the Spirit descend from heaven like a dove, and it remained on him.*

¹¹ Ephesians 4:30: *And do not grieve the Holy Spirit of God, by whom you were sealed for the day of redemption*; 1 Thessalonians 5:19: *Do not quench the Spirit.*

¹² C. S. Lewis, *Mere Christianity*, MacMillan Publishing Co., Inc., New York, 1960. p. 141.

¹³ John 15:26: *But when the Helper comes, whom I will send to you from the Father, the Spirit of truth, who proceeds from the Father, he will bear witness about me.*

¹⁴ Isaiah 30:15: *In returning and rest you shall be saved; in quietness and in trust shall be your strength*; Isaiah 64:4: *From of old no one has heard or perceived by the ear, no eye has seen a God besides you, who acts for those who wait for him*; John 6:29: *Jesus answered them, "This is the work of God, that you believe in him whom he has sent."*

Chapter 13: Ministry to Others

¹ Matthew 22:39-40: *And a second is like it: You shall love your neighbor as yourself.*

² Matthew 6:33: *But seek first the kingdom of God and his righteousness, and all these things will be added to you.*

³ John 12:26: *If anyone serves me, he must follow me.*

⁴ This passage from 1 Samuel gives us insight into the focus of the Lord which is evidently not on the externals which so enthrall us, but on the hidden depths of the heart: 1 Samuel 16:7: *For the Lord sees not as man sees... the Lord looks on the heart.*

⁵ I kept this quote on my office wall for years, but cannot find it now to give it a proper citation. If you know where I can find it, please email me at info@forerunners4him.org.

⁶ The Lord is behind those open doors. In the beginning open doors for ministering are usually from Him. As we grow, more discernment may be required, but He seems to like to get us started with many wide open options: Revelation 3:7: *The holy one... who opens and no one will shut, who shuts and no one opens.*

⁷ Every one of us—from the least to the greatest—receives "gifts" from God for doing ministry. See Chapters 13-16 for more on God's gifts for life and service.

⁸ Forgiving "from the heart" is the Lord's own standard for us: Matthew 18:32-35: *So also my heavenly Father will do to every one of you, if you do not forgive your brother from your heart.*

⁹ The Lord guarantees that His saving help will come to us in any situation in which we call on Him for help: Romans 10:13: *Everyone who calls on the name of the Lord will be saved.*

¹⁰ John 13:15-17: *I have given you an example that you also should do just as I have done to you.*

¹¹ Ephesians 4:15-16: *We are to grow up in every way into him who is the head.*

Chapter 14: Preparing for Ministry

[1] Love is our "marching order." We are never to "break ranks" by falling out of love: John 13:34-35: *A new commandment I give to you, that you love one another...*

[2] Matthew 6:3-4: *And your Father who sees in secret will reward you.*

[3] Jesus doesn't hesitate to command us to love at all times and in all situations. There is no time when these two commands don't apply: Mark 12:28-31: *You shall love the Lord your God with all your heart... you shall love your neighbor.*

[4] By the sheer number of times compassion is recorded we should be alerted to what a key motivator it was for the Lord: Matthew 9:36, 14:14, 15:32: Mark 6:34, 8:2, 9:22; Luke 7:13, 10:33; 15:20. Here is one example: Mark 8:1-2: *I have compassion on the crowd...*

[5] 1 Peter 5:6-7: *Humble yourselves, therefore, under the mighty hand of God...*

[6] While it is true that leaders will be judged "with greater strictness" this doesn't mean that the Lord has less mercy, love or forgiveness available to them. Besides, in assuring us that He will indeed judge them, He wants us leave that work to Him, not take it on ourselves: James 3:1: *We who teach will be judged with greater strictness.*

[7] Jesus' parable about forgiveness illustrates the seriousness of God on this matter: Matthew 18:32-35: *You wicked servant... should not you have had mercy on your fellow servant, as I had mercy on you?*

[8] 1 Peter 1:8-9 KJV: *Yet believing, ye rejoice with joy unspeakable and full of glory...*

[9] The principle here is that those who truly seek, shall truly find: Matthew 7:7-8 AMP: *For everyone who keeps on asking receives; and he who keeps on seeking finds;* and John 7:17 AMP: *If any man desires to do His will (God's pleasure), he will know...*

[10] John 15:12-15: *No longer do I call you servants... I have called you friends...*

[11] John 14:15: *If you love me, you will keep my commandments.*

[12] Colossians 3:15: *And let the peace of Christ rule in your hearts...*

[13] Hebrews 13:17: *Obey your leaders and submit to them...*

Chapter 15: Calling and Purpose

[1] Paul says that in "all things" God is working towards His ultimate purpose which is our glorification as true "sons" who display all that is in Jesus. We are "called" by God to be as loving as Jesus (among other things) and God Himself will accomplish it: Romans 8:28-30: *He also predestined to be conformed to the image of his Son.*

[2] 2 Corinthians 5:14-15: *That those who live might no longer live for themselves.*

[3] If you need help learning how to love and accept yourself the way God does, then please see "Love Thyself" at www.healingstreamsusa.org.

[4] There are three points to the story of the "Good Samaritan" that we don't want to miss: 1) Jesus told it in answer to a question about the second commandment (just what we are examining here), 2) our "neighbor" is anyone in need, and 3) love is compassion for human suffering *in action.* Jesus didn't praise the Samaritan because he felt love, but because he *did* love. See Luke 25-37.

[5] Philippians 3:7-8: *The surpassing worth of knowing Christ Jesus my Lord.*

[6] Having worked with addicts and people "on the streets" for over 20 years, I have been shown countless scars and told unnerving tales of escapes from certain death, all ending with "I know God is keeping me alive for a reason." Naturally, I ask what that reason is. *No one* has yet to tell me. They all say they don't know. That's when I take them to these

two commands to help them understand what God is up to in their lives. It's great good fun to turn the lights on with God's help. What hangs things up is that initially they always see purpose as service to others, never as truly knowing and loving God.

[7] Putting Jesus first ensures that the other things will fall into place: Matthew 6:33: *Seek first the kingdom of God and his righteousness, and all these things will be added to you.*

[8] As a pastor and former missionary, I have heard these stories told two ways: 1) after years of running from God's call, the wilderness weary soul finally caves in, opens up, surrenders and then hears the Lord say: "But I was never asking you to do that or go there!" *or*, 2) the surrendered one is sent where he/she feared and ends up loving it!

[9] By the way, intellectuals who had a "head" love for humanity in general terms have been the scourge of humanity in practical terms: Lenin, Stalin, Mao Zedong, Pol Pot, Castro, etc. We would have all been better off if they had grown compassion, rather than ideas.

[10] Acts 16:9-10: *And a vision appeared to Paul in the night: a man of Macedonia...*

[11] Weaknesses will always help you work with humility and compassion, if you let them. They are great for drawing us back to the Lord in brokenness and surrender, but they are not gifts for service! Thank God, we are usually called on the basis of what feel like strengths. However, fears are different. Your strength may be teaching, but you are afraid of speaking in public. Do it anyway!

[12] Proverbs 4:23: *Keep your heart with all vigilance, for from it flow the springs of life.*

[13] Psalms 42:7: *Deep calls to deep at the roar of your waterfalls...*

[14] Being a pastor, I know that there are special challenges and temptations which confuse the issue of living for Jesus in the midst of serving the church. "Religious" traditions and spiritual misconceptions abound. It is, after all, a profession that the enemy has been attacking for centuries.

Chapter 16: The School of the Spirit

[1] Holy Spirit's task is to lead us into nothing less than all truth: John 16:12-13: *When the Spirit of truth comes, he will guide you into all the truth...*; Much of what He has to teach us is beyond our unaided ability to understand: Isaiah 55:9: *For as the heavens are higher than the earth, so are my ways higher than your ways and my thoughts than your thoughts.*

[2] In saying the Lord is "our most devoted critic" I am not saying that He is critical of us, or faults us, or blames us, or condemns us. Only that He does have a steady and at times disturbing way of pointing out what we are doing wrong.

[3] All condemnation comes from the enemy, also known as the "Accuser": Revelation 12:10: *The accuser of our brothers has been thrown down, who accuses them day and night.*

[4] John 15:4-5: *Abide in me, and I in you. ...for apart from me you can do nothing.*

[5] The writer of Hebrews is quoting Psalm 40:7, but describing Jesus: Hebrews 10:7: *Behold, I have come to do your will, O God...*

[6] Just one tantalizing example: Isaiah 40:31: *But they who wait for the Lord shall renew their strength... they shall run and not be weary; they shall walk and not faint.*

[7] Hebrews 4:3: *For we who have believed enter that rest;* Luke 21:19 KJV: *In your patience possess ye your souls.*

[8] Weaknesses are not sins. Being easily tired is a weakness. Having a debilitating injury is a weakness. God can easily work around these. Even weakness in the face of temptation is not a sin, but giving in to the temptation is sin.

[9] Luke 2:49 MKJV: *Do you not know that I must be about my Father's business?*

[10] Matthew 11:28-30: *Take my yoke upon you… For my yoke is easy, and my burden is light.*
[11] Isaiah 45:22: *Turn to me and be saved… For I am God, and there is no other.*
[12] We don't have power to redeem anyone's life, not even our own: Psalm 49:6-9: *Truly no man can ransom another, or give to God the price of his life.*
[13] James 4:13-15: *Instead you ought to say, "If the Lord wills, we will live and do this or that."*
[14] Ephesians 5:21: *Submitting to one another out of reverence for Christ;* Ephesians 4:1-3: *Bearing with one another in love, eager to maintain the unity of the Spirit in the bond of peace.*
[15] Philippians 2:2-5: *Let each of you look not only to his own interests, but also to the interests of others…*
[16] Peter calls them "fiery" trials. What makes a trial "fiery" may be the higher level of suffering in it, or the fear it arouses in us that we may lose our salvation (and "burn") because of it—something that will never happen if we persevere through the trial: 1 Peter 4:12: *Beloved, do not be surprised at the fiery trial when it comes upon you to test you…*
[17] It is a "strange" work, because it makes it seem that God is upset with us and because the One who loves us is actually allowing pain to come into our lives—just the opposite of what we would expect: Hebrews 12:11: *For the moment all discipline seems painful rather than pleasant, but later it yields the peaceful fruit of righteousness.*

Chapter 17: Talent, Fruit and Gifts

[1] James 1:17-18: *Every good gift and every perfect gift is from above…*
[2] Musical abilities and fluency with languages are examples of abilities that flourish best if cultivated early.
[3] Practical wisdom, patience and foresight are examples of abilities that grow later in life for many people, even those who are not Christian.
[4] The critical issue of our separation from God is a deeper issue than what we do; it goes to the depth of who we are as fallen beings: We not only sin, we have a sin nature. While it is true that we can never do sufficient good deeds to counterbalance what is wrong with us (our sins and sinfulness), the Bible never takes the position that we cannot do good deeds. In fact the whole point of instruction in the law and the holiness of God is to draw out of us (whenever it is possible) better choices and better deeds. Right from the beginning we see the Lord entreating Cain to do good: Genesis 4:6-7: *And if you do not do well, sin is crouching at the door. Its desire is for you, but you must rule over it.*
[5] Righteousness can be used to mean either our standing with God (which is only made righteous through faith in Christ), or our actual deeds which may or may not be righteous depending upon what they are, as well as our motives in doing them. The Reformers called this second category "practical righteousness" and they expected it to be the natural outcome of people who have received the gift of justification, or "positional righteousness" in their standing with God. However, many converts have shown that a person can have positional righteousness and very little practical righteousness to go with it; and many an unbeliever has demonstrated that they can have a good deal of practical righteousness without having positional righteousness at all. Go figure! Perhaps more discipline from the Lord is needed: Hebrews 12:11: *Later it yields the peaceful fruit of righteousness to those who have been trained by it.*
[6] Galatians 5:22 *But the fruit of the Spirit is…*

[7] There are specific kinds or levels of peace and joy which are unique to us through our faith relationship with Jesus, such as the peace of Christ and the joy of our salvation, but peace and joy in general are in some form known to all.

Chapter 18: Five Ministry Gifts

[1] Constantine the Great (272-337 AD) was the Roman Emperor who first declared that Christianity would no longer be persecuted and who was himself a believer. His Edict of Milan (313 AD) proclaimed tolerance for Christians throughout the Empire.

[2] This was brought to a head by the controversy surrounding Montanism. The prophets of the movement needed to submit to the instruction of those with more balance and wisdom. Unfortunately, the bishops who opposed them and successfully suppressed the movement were not themselves gifted charismatically. They didn't understand prophecy (as an apostle would have) and hence could not appreciate what the movement represented or be respected by those who had what they were lacking.

[3] It was Jesus who named demonic deliverance a gift suitable for children: Matthew 15:22-26: *It is not right to take the children's bread and throw it to the dogs…*

[4] This is not to disparage pastors. I have been one for years and have tremendous respect for those I know. Theirs is a high and holy calling and immensely difficult. But they are not the leaders of first rank: That place belongs to the (missing) apostles and prophets!

[5] 2 Corinthians 12:12: *The signs of a true apostle… with signs and wonders and mighty works.*

[6] In Acts 19:1-7 we have "disciples" who "believed" in Jesus, yet lacked the Holy Spirit baptism and supernatural gifts which accompany it. Paul wouldn't leave it at that and neither should we: *And when Paul had laid his hands on them, the Holy Spirit came on them, and they began speaking in tongues and prophesying.*

[7] Acts 18:24-26 is a picture of a Christian teacher (Apollos) being further instructed in the baptism of the Holy Spirit, since he only knew the "baptism of John" which is of water and points towards faith in Christ, not the empowerment of the Spirit: *He spoke and taught accurately the things concerning Jesus, though he knew only the baptism of John.*

[8] Jesus is the ultimate and actual "head of the Church," but He obviously confers "headship" to leaders in the church.

[9] So important was the concept of the chosen twelve that Judas was quickly replaced (after his betrayal and death) by Matthias: Acts 1:24-26

[10] 2 Corinthians 11:13: *False apostles… disguising themselves as apostles of Christ.*

[11] Acts 15:6: *The apostles and the elders were gathered… to consider this matter.*

[12] 2 Corinthians 12:12 AMP: *The signs that indicate a [genuine] apostle were performed among you fully… in miracles and wonders and mighty works.*

[13] 1 Corinthians 14:24-25: *If all prophesy… the secrets of his heart are disclosed.*

[14] See Hebrews 12: 18-24 for a striking image of this difference.

[15] Nahum 1:15: *Behold… the feet of him who brings good news…*

[16] Colossians 1:5-7: *The gospel… has come to you, as indeed in the whole world…*

[17] On the road to Emmaus Easter morning two unsuspecting disciples discovered that Jesus had been in the midst: Luke 24:32: *They said to each other, "Did not our hearts burn within us while he talked to us on the road, while he opened to us the Scriptures?"*

Chapter 19: Seven Motivational Gifts

[1] Notice that God is at work in us to "will" and "to do." He is giving us the desires and providing us with abilities in carrying them out: Philippians 2:12-13: *For it is God who works in you, both to will and to work for his good pleasure.*

[2] The Holy Spirit has been "with us" since conception. He has always been our Teacher and life coach whether we knew it or not. It's just that until conversion, He had to stay on the outside and couldn't teach us the things of the Lord, or of the spiritual life as He now does *within* us: John 14:16-17: *You know him, for he dwells with you and will be in you.*

[3] Colossians 3:15: *And let the peace of Christ rule in your hearts.*

[4] Proverbs 3:5-6: *Trust in the Lord with all your heart... and he will make straight your paths.*

[5] Romans 8:12-14: Notice that we have to put aside the flesh in order to be led by the Spirit: *But if by the Spirit you put to death the deeds of the body, you will live.*

[6] Galatians 5:16-17: This is the spiritual "tug of war" which goes on in every Christian's life: *The desires of the flesh are against the Spirit, and... the Spirit are against the flesh.*

[7] Acts 2:42-43: *And they devoted themselves to the apostles' teaching...*

Chapter 20: Nine Gifts of Power

[1] Just as the Lord promised through Malachi, He opens windows in heaven and pours out a blessing. As great as the blessing on tithing is, the "outpouring" of the Spirit is even greater (see Chapter 7, "The Baptism of Power"): Malachi 3:10: *Bring the full tithes into the storehouse... I will... pour down for you a blessing until there is no more need.*

[2] The charismatic experience of the Corinthian church was by no means unusual. In the first two centuries of the church these nine operations of supernatural power flourished along with the baptism of the Spirit which enabled their widespread growth. The Early Church was fully charismatic across the whole Mediterranean basin! The rare exception would have been a church lacking in these two features as modern scholarship has abundantly demonstrated. See Kilian McDonnel and George T. Montague, *Christian Initiation and Baptism in the Holy Spirit*, The Liturgical Press, Collegeville, Minnesota; 1990.

[3] Other gifts include the "ministerial" gifts or offices listed in Ephesians 4:11: apostles, prophets, evangelists, pastors, and teachers; the "motivational" gifts for service listed in Romans 12:6-8: prophesy, service, teaching, exhortation, giving, mercy, and administration; and gifts individually mentioned: hospitality, intercession, missionary, exorcism, music, craftsmanship, and celibacy. Even natural talents and abilities are gifts from God and can be placed under His leadership in service through Him to others. Ultimately, every good gift comes from the Father, so all genuine gifts have a spiritual Source and connection.

[4] James 1:5: *If any of you lacks wisdom, let him ask God... it will be given him.*

[5] Saving faith is described in Romans 10:13 and Ephesians 2:8-9: *By grace you have been saved through faith... not your own doing; it is the gift of God.*

[6] Jesus said that our primary "work" is to cultivate our faith—the gift of faith in Him that we have been given. It is understood by the Lord that most of our faith in Him (or for what He has promised to do) is something that we will have to work at maintaining: John 6:28-29: *This is the work of God, that you believe in him whom he has sent.*

[7] Two obvious exceptions to this sweeping general statement would be the raising of people out of death and the recreation of organs or other body parts, both of which have been occurring in our day in surprising numbers.

[8] 1 Corinthians 13:1: *If I speak in the tongues of men and of angels…*

[9] Acts 2:4-7: *They were bewildered, because each one was hearing them speak in his own language.*

[10] My friend, Eddy Browning, who brought me to the Lord had a dead-on prophetic gift as well as discerning of spirits (I had seven demons cast out of me the night of my conversion). It was his gift of tongues combined with the interpretation of tongues that came to my rescue many times in the early years of my growth in Christ. I would call Eddy on the phone and lay out my trouble. He would pray in tongues; then when the interpretation came forth, I was set free by some insight it conveyed, and was fully satisfied I had heard from the Lord!

Chapter 21: Doing Ministry

[1] When faith in Christ is rising in us, all is glorious: Colossians 1:27: *…The riches of the glory of this mystery, which is Christ in you, the hope of glory.*

[2] Paul describes this cycle in its extreme form: 2 Corinthians 4:11-12: *So death is at work in us, but life in you.*

[3] 1 Peter 5:6-7: *Casting all your anxieties on him, because he cares for you.*

[4] Notice how slight the action indicated by the Lord and how great His approval of it as a way of ministering of love: Mark 9:36-37: *Whoever receives one such child in my name receives me;* Mark 9:41: *Whoever gives you a cup of water to drink… will by no means lose his reward.*

[5] Galatians 5:22-23: *But the fruit of the Spirit is love, joy, peace, patience, kindness, goodness, faithfulness, gentleness, self-control…*

[6] Matthew 12:33-35: *The good person out of his good treasure brings forth good…*

[7] John 4:35-36: *Lift up your eyes, and see that the fields are white for harvest.*

[8] 1 Corinthians 13:1-3: *But have not love… I gain nothing.*

[9] Romans 10:13 For *"everyone who calls on the name of the Lord will be saved."*

[10] Hebrews 4:16: *Let us then with confidence draw near to the throne of grace…*

[11] Psalms 16:9: *In your presence there is fullness of joy…*

[12] In consecrating the work to the Lord, we should allow the Holy Spirit to examine our motives to ensure that our true desire is to serve the Lord, not any agenda of our own: Luke 16:13: *No servant can serve two masters…*

[13] Colossians 3:15: *And let the peace of Christ rule in your hearts…*

[14] Isaiah 30:15" *For thus said the Lord God, the Holy One of Israel, "In returning and rest you shall be saved; in quietness and in trust shall be your strength."*

Chapter 22: The Heart of a Servant

[1] See Matthew 20:20-28 for the full passage.

[2] Lowest because most fallen. In rising upwards into unbridled pride, the Lucifer fell into the depths of depravity, becoming Satan, the one who opposes God.

[3] This is the paradox: He is our Head, but He also takes the lowest place of serving us, His Body: Colossians 1:17-18: *And he is the head of the body, the church…*

[4] John Michael Talbot has many CD's. The lyrics are powerful; the music is beautiful. "Nature and Grace" is on an album from his early period, *No Longer Strangers.*

[5] This is written about Jesus who now lives with this same desire on the inside of us: Hebrews 10:7: *Then I said, 'Behold, I have come to do your will, O God, as it is written.'*

[6] Hebrews 12:1-2: *Who for the joy that was set before him endured the cross...*

[7] Luke 9:23: *Let him deny himself and take up his cross daily and follow me.*

[8] See the letters of Paul (Romans, Galatians, Philippians, Colossians, and Titus), James, 2 Peter, and Jude. NKJV renders the title "bondservants."

[9] John 15:13-15: *No longer do I call you servants... but I have called you friends.*

[10] The "Big Five" connectors to Jesus are Bible, prayer, worship, fellowship and service. Do these regularly and the Lord will use them as "safety nets" to keep drawing you back to Himself whenever you stray, or to help hold you fast in case of an attack.

[11] If you feel your love for Him waning, go to Him to get it back. Our love for God is not a feeling that comes from us. It is what happens in us when we see His love: 1 John 4:19 AMP: *We love Him, because He first loved us.*

[12] Isaiah 30:15: *In returning and rest you shall be saved...*

[13] Acts 3:19: *Repent... that times of refreshing may come from the presence of the Lord.*

[14] Exodus 33:13-15: *If your presence will not go with me, do not bring us up from here.*

[15] I put that there for myself: I don't feel that I am especially good at anything I am pursuing, but I am doggedly determined to keep seeking Him for guidance and direction in all my ways. He blesses that right intention and seems to make up the difference. He will do the same for you!

Chapter 23: The Care of Souls

[1] Obviously, I'm not suggesting that they should be allowed to do illegal things to us, like assault us, or steal from us. But verbal abuse? At our mission (the Old Savannah City Mission in Savannah, GA) we reign in abusive and offensive language, but we work at not letting it get to us; otherwise, we would be going off on them! Jesus said that there is a blessing to reap when we are verbally abused. It is well worth learning how to reap: Matthew 5:11-12: *Blessed are you when others revile you and persecute you and utter all kinds of evil against you falsely on my account.*

[2] "Soul" is a term that has wide and rich usage in the Bible, but no clearly established definition. General agreement has it that we are spirit, soul and body and that the soul is composed of intellect, emotion and will. The heart is the deepest part of the soul.

[3] Mark 12:31: *The second is this: 'You shall love your neighbor as yourself.'*

[4] Scripture is clear that this is what we are meant to do by way of comforting others: Romans 12:15-16: *Rejoice with those who rejoice, weep with those who weep...*

[5] 1 Corinthians 12:22-26: *But God has so composed the body, giving greater honor to the part that lacked it... but that the members may have the same care for one another.*

[6] Two brothers were praised for covering their father's nakedness: Genesis 9:20-23: *Shem and Japheth... Their faces were turned backward, and they did not see their father's nakedness.*

[7] Showing respect is very Biblical: Romans 13:7: *Pay to all what is owed to them... respect to whom respect is owed, honor to whom honor is owed.*

[8] Many books have been written about St. Francis, but the best is a collection made shortly after he died. Part history, part fable, you have to do a bit of sorting it out, but the images it gives us of this remarkable man are indelible: *The Little Flowers of St. Francis.*

Chapter 24: The Art of Listening

[1] Hippocrates, the father of Western medicine, included in the famous "Hippocratic Oath" that all doctors take a promise to do no harm: "With regard to healing the sick, I will devise and order for them the best diet, according to my judgment and means; and I will take care that they suffer no hurt or damage."

[2] Even so, being a good listener is essential for becoming good in any other area of ministry.

[3] See Exodus 3:1-4:17 for the complete story.

[4] James 4:13-15: *Say, "If the Lord wills, we will live and do this or that."*

[5] Romans 5:4-5: *God's love has been poured into our hearts through the Holy Spirit.*

[6] James 1:19-20: *Let every person be quick to hear, slow to speak, slow to anger…*

[7] Romans 12:15-16: *Rejoice with those who rejoice, weep with those who weep…*

[8] 2 Corinthians 1:3-5: *So that we may be able to comfort those who are in any affliction, with the comfort with which we ourselves are comforted by God.*

[9] Hebrews 13:1-2: *Do not neglect to show hospitality to strangers…*

FORERUNNER MINISTRIES

Which hope we have as an anchor of the soul,
both sure and steadfast, and which enters into that within the veil,
where the Forerunner has entered for us, even Jesus.
Hebrews 6: 19-20a MKJV

THE eCOURSE FOR HEALING
www.HealingStreamsusa.org

Practically everyone needs recovery of their heart from some painful issues of the past or could readily benefit from gaining mastery over their emotional turbulence in the present. The peace of Christ is meant to be a river of life that we experience all day long—no matter what our circumstances may be. Let the 24 main healing lessons and workout sessions of our free eCourse for Healing take your heart on pilgrimage to a place called the Kingdom of God that is already right inside you.

SPIRIT FILLED LIVING IN CHRIST
www.Forerunners4Him.org

Whether you are a brand new recruit or a "seasoned veteran," if you find that your peace levels are slipping and your joy is not full, then everything on this site is designed to help you come into the fullness of what it truly means to be saved by grace through faith—in all of your days and all of your situations. For us a forerunner is anyone who receives salvation and begins a lifetime quest of "running" into the Heart of God for intimacy and "going before the Lord" to prepare His way into other lives. That's your heart too, isn't it? Come get the equipping you need to be a liberated lover of Jesus and a loving liberator of others.

SANE AND SENSIBLE PERSPECTIVES
www.TheLastDays.info

Many people these days have a God-given hunger to know more about the Last Days. You'll find a feast at this website! Savor the taste of these "sane and sensible perspectives" which are salted with humor and spiced with fresh insights. We have extensive sections devoted to Signs of His Coming, When Is the Rapture, Crucial Components, and Ways to Prepare along with free downloads, an Updates section and blog. Best of all, an entire six-hundred-page commentary on The Book of Revelation is available for free reading and chapter by chapter download.

BOOKS FROM FORERUNNER

If you enjoyed this book, you can purchase copies for friends and keep exploring the spiritual life through these other insightful books by Steve Evans, available in paperback and eBook at Amazon.com.

The Book of Revelation takes you on a verse-by-verse stroll through the most complex prophetic vision ever given. These "sane and sensible perspectives" are guaranteed to help you see what this amazing book is trying to show us. With this detailed overview, you'll have the insights you'll need for the days to come.
624 pages. Paperback: $22.00. Kindle: $3.99.

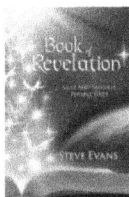

Matters of the Heart is a 24 lesson workbook designed to guide Christian believers through the basic understandings necessary for releasing emotional damage from the past and gaining a grace-based restoration to wholeness. Each chapter is filled with "tools" for practical application.
278 pages. Paperback: $20.00.

The Missing Peace includes all of the 24 lessons of the *Matters of the Heart* teaching series, but without the workbook's other material, focusing instead on a stream of scriptural revelation that will show you how to bring your heart to God and receive His Heart for you in return.
194 pages. Paperback: $15.00.

Rescued from Hell chronicles one man's journey into a ten year living nightmare and his astonishing true story of return. Was it an insane delusion or a satanic deception? This is a tale both incredible and terrible, yet studded with life affirming humor and hope-filled insights into the spiritual realities that surround us.
190 pages. Paperback: $12.50.

An Illustrated Guide to the Spiritual Life captures in living color with playful insights the otherwise elusive, invisible realities of our life in God. This "illustrated devotional" includes explanations, scriptures and prayers. It is written for the general reader, but is also a pictorial companion to *The Missing Peace*.
126 pages. Paperback: $17.50.
The River of Peace Series, Vol. 1.

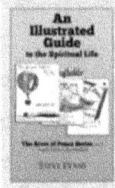

Good Grief is not for everyone, but for those who despite their pain have "set their hearts on pilgrimage", determined to make it to the other side of the Valley of Tears, allowing sorrow that is *rightly* carried to mend their hearts and guide their lives toward God's new beginning.
70 pages. Paperback: $10.00.
The River of Peace Series, Vol. 2.

Salvation Basics provides easy to understand answers to life's most important questions: "What will happen to me when I die?" and "What can I do about it?" You will not only discover God's grace-filled way for getting you to heaven, but also His "secret" for living the heavenly life down here.

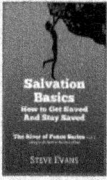

118 pages. Paperback: $10.00.
The River of Peace Series, Vol. 3.

Ministry Basics will prepare you to launch into the sea of human need, lostness and misery which surrounds you, finding your place in the Rescue and your highest path of purpose at the Lord's side. Let these field-tested truths equip you for a joy-filled lifetime of Holy Spirit empowered ministry.

163 pages. Paperback: $10.00.
The River of Peace Series, Vol. 4.

Knowing God may surprise you. The invisible God can be truly, intimately and delightfully known. But it gets even better because there are not just One of Him to get to know, but Three. Think of this as a guide book, not an encyclopedia. Three amazing Persons already know you and love you. What are you waiting for?

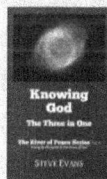

161 pages. Paperback: $10.00.
The River of Peace Series, Vol. 5.

Knowing Jesus will introduce you to the God-Man. He is far and away the most wonderful Person in the universe to know. And He can be known! Simply opening one's heart to Him is all He needs for that life-long adventure to begin. Let this "Spiritual Biography" lead you into fresh revelations of key moments in His life.

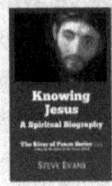

159 pages. Paperback: $10.00.

The River of Peace Series, Vol. 6.

Knowing the Spirit will introduce you to the Mystery Person of the Trinity, help you recognize His ways and connect with His presence, so that you can live with greater delight in His guidance and power. Let this book give you eyes to see and ears to hear your inner Guest as He works with you each day.

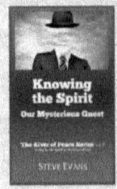

149 pages. Paperback: $10.00.

The River of Peace Series, Vol. 7.

Holy Spirit explores practical ways of getting to know the One who supplies us with supernatural power for life and ministry. Why should the Person of the Trinity who lives within us be so mysterious to us? This book combines *Knowing the Spirit* with *Ministry Basics* in a single, sensational volume.

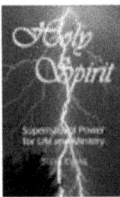

171 pages. Paperback: $15.00.

Jesus: An Intimate Portrait will give you fresh perspectives on His Story—the heroic story of the One who shapes all human history by His life and Word. Let these intimate insights reveal the living, breathing God-Man in ways you never encountered Him before. Seeing Him changes everything!

212 pages. Paperback: $15.00.

ABOUT THE AUTHOR

Steve Evans came to faith as one brought back from the dead after a decade of occult oppression and torment. His passion is to see people everywhere released from past brokenness and fully equipped for life and ministry. At HealingStreamsUSA.org he teaches believers how to recover their emotional freedom and master their inward state. At Forerunners4Him.org he shows how to live in the presence and power of the Spirit. His newest website, TheLastDays.info, gives "sane and sensible perspectives" on the events of the Last Days that are heading our way.

Steve has authored numerous books, including: *The Missing Peace, The Book of Revelation, Salvation Basics, Ministry Basics, Knowing the Spirit* and *Rescued from Hell* which tells the story of his own harrowing descent into inner darkness and ultimate restoration. Steve is an ordained minister and a former carpenter, craftsman and missionary.

www.ingramcontent.com/pod-product-compliance
Lightning Source LLC
Chambersburg PA
CBHW051832090426
42736CB00011B/1767